Flower
Arranging
for
Period
Decoration

Flower Arranging for Period Decoration

by Marian Klamkin

Photographs by Charles Klamkin

AVENEL BOOKS · NEW YORK

Contents

Contents

*Flower
Arranging
for
Period
Decoration*

1

Arranging Flowers
in the Home

A true test of good design in
the decorative arts can be made by asking: Is a fashion
pleasing to live with and have in one's home and is it com-
plementary to the room for which it was made or purchased?
Today's upsurge in styles of the past may be a denial of the
cold, modern style which has dominated our furnishings
and architecture for two decades. Because there is relatively
little that is new or different in most modern home furnishings, more and more frequently furniture of many past eras
is being reproduced and adapted to modern living. A great
variety of antique reproductions are being combined with
authentic old pieces, and old fabrics and wallpaper prints
are being copied and adapted. We speak of decorating a
new home or apartment in "Early American," "French Empire," or "French Provincial." Good design of any period is
never lost, but is copied and adapted again and again.

Most small decorative antiques have become so popular with modern collectors that they are extremely rare and high-priced, but china or pottery that was well designed and pleasing to look at in past centuries is being faithfully copied in new versions, so that accessories for period decoration are readily available to complement our furnishings and to add a tone of warmth to modern decor. One is fortunate indeed to own an authentic Early American pine knife box or an antique Wedgwood bowl, but good replicas of these and dozens of other period accessories are available now, and their decorative effect in a room is essentially the same as when the originals are used, for usually only the best period design is copied.

Good examples are the authentic reproductions from Colonial Williamsburg, the Henry Ford Museum, and many other places in our country. Study museum pieces before going out to shop, and you will be guided to the proper selection of decorative accessories.

When we consider flower arrangements as decorative accessories for the home, we have little literature of the past from which to draw. Flower arranging, an art form popular in the Western world only since the beginning of this century, has now become firmly established with garden clubs in almost every town in England and America. These clubs hold competitions for best designs in various categories. Unfortunately, the most important aspect of flower arranging seems to have been forgotten: a good arrangement, made to be used in a room setting, should harmonize with and enhance the furnishings and space around it. To make an arrangement of fresh flowers for other people to judge and admire until the petals begin to fall seems to us an unfor-

The deep purple of these irises is the same color as the border of the Victorian plate. The arrangement has been designed to include the plate as an integral part of the overall composition

tunate waste of time and effort. To use flower arrangements as room decoration, whether fresh, dried, or artificial, is an ever-recurring joy. The arrangements should be coordinated with the room in which they are to be placed. The container should be compatible with the period, the proportions should be pleasing, and the colors should be chosen with care.

As there is no guide to tell us what type of arrangement will best suit a particular style this book will begin by discussing the choice of flower containers for each period. It will be necessary also to trace the development of the

3

various furniture styles. As the arrangements will become an intrinsic part of the room for which they were created, many of them will be made of lasting flowers, both artificial and dried. Most of these arrangements can be adapted to fresh flowers, using the same types of containers and the same basic designs.

The present trend in floral arrangements for home decoration is away from the stiff formal types one sees at flower shows and in many magazines. No one should have to labor over an arrangement of fresh flowers in order to enjoy their beauty. In many of our illustrations of fresh flower arrangements, there seldom will be more than two or three different types of plant material used together. Not many home gardeners today have room for a wide variety of flowers, and chances are that only a few kinds of cut flowers will be available to most arrangers at one time during the growing season. For those who enjoy fresh flowers in the house during the summer, the incentive to cut and use them is greater if one does not feel compelled to spend a long time arranging them for a few days of enjoyment.

Many of the arrangements illustrated will be comprised of lasting material, dried, paper, or plastic. Other "flowers" will be made of feathers, beads, or any other material which seems to be correct for the container used and the period for which the arrangement is designed. If an Art Nouveau vase is so decorative in its glaze and shape that flowers detract from it, often a few peacock feathers will give the proper touch. In addition to the realistic plastic flowers, fruit, and foliage now available, there are many varieties and sizes of paper flowers which add a bright note and are compatible

*An ironstone tureen is enhanced when used uncovered
as a container for this lasting arrangement of artificial
daisies and bachelor's buttons*

with many periods of interior design. It is hoped that the
arrangements shown in this book will suggest other ideas for
arranging in antique or modern containers that the reader
might already own. They might also lead to a hobby of
collecting artificial flowers composed of various materials
which were made in the past and used in one form or another for many years; these can be found in variety all over
the world.

There are numerous sources from which one may learn
about period furniture, and the many museums with display
rooms of various periods will help guide us in our choice of
furniture, fabrics, and accessories for our homes. Most of us
cannot hope to own authentic antiques of the periods in

which we are interested—the cost and scarcity of good antiques will prohibit this—but we are able to purchase authentic reproductions of furniture which have proved to be enduring and in good taste. Frequently, the new is combined with the old to give warmth to modern architecture. Many young couples, as they discover that primitive American furniture often costs no more than new contemporary pieces, spend their spare time hunting for and refinishing such a piece as an old dry sink or spice chest that they feel can only increase in value as the years go by. The addition of the right type of flower arrangement will enhance this kind of furniture and give added warmth and beauty to their room.

In order to place our illustrated arrangements in their proper settings, a short introduction is given the furniture and backgrounds typical of each period. Because the containers shown are antiques or reproductions of period pieces, decorative accessories of each period will be discussed. Usually, those of us who are interested in flower arranging are also interested in antiques; we haunt antique shops, auctions, and "flea markets" looking for interesting containers for our arrangements. Therefore, this book is also a guide for choosing the proper container. There are many dishes and other utensils which, although not particularly decorative in themselves, make excellent flower containers for a room decorated in period style. Look for tureens minus covers, wooden boxes and bowls which, while not functional for fresh flower arrangements, are good for dried materials, and cracked containers of all types in which a long-lasting arrangement might look pleasing and conceal the flaws. Often, original antiques with flaws such as these can be purchased for very little and add much to the decoration of a room.

One's idea of beauty is personal and individual. No two people furnish a home in the same way. Given identical houses and furniture, two different women will change the interiors until their individual personalities are reflected in their homes. In these days of "tract houses" and identical apartments, it becomes even more essential for us to make our homes represent our own interests and personalities. We can do this through our choice of color for the background, furniture, and accessories. Flowers and plants are as important a part of room accessories as pottery and china, and when tastefully combined they give the home the individuality, warmth, and color that one strives for.

2

Mechanics of
Flower Arranging

With some basic knowledge of design and color, almost anyone can put flowers in a vase in a way that will look reasonably pleasing. Making period flower arrangements requires a knowledge of the type of arrangement that complements the room in which the arrangement is to be placed. Garden clubs, through their complex rules, have placed an aura about the art of flower arranging that tends to make the amateur feel that the art is an esoteric one, and too difficult to learn. Therefore, the alternative is either to do without arrangements in the home or slave to make them strictly according to the rules of design and proportion mandatory for the flower shows and carried over, unfortunately, into home displays.

The rules of proportion by which flower arrangements are judged at flower shows are sometimes helpful to those who must work within a set style in order to have confidence in their results. However, when making arrangements that are intended to coordinate with a particular period of the decorative arts before this century, one may keep in mind simply the basic style of the period and attempt to create a design representative of that time. Outside of Japan, there were no set rules governing flower arrangements before the twentieth century. Therefore, except when making flower arrangements that are to be representative of this century, we must look to the furniture, small decorative antiques, and the paintings and prints of each period in order to create an arrangement in a style that will harmonize with it. At the same time, we must keep in mind the total picture of the room in which the arrangement is to be placed.

Flower arrangements made to go with furnishings of periods prior to the end of the nineteenth century (when the interest in things Japanese became important) will be bouquets of one kind or another. Flowers were not wired or tied together for arrangements before the Art Nouveau period and the pinholder is a fairly new invention adapted from the Japanese. The container and the available flowers usually dictated the type of arrangement, but as tastes changed over the centuries, flower bouquets in Europe and America changed along with the other decorative arts. We can make life more interesting as we learn some of the background of particular periods and also broaden our taste and knowledge.

CHOOSING MATERIALS FOR ARRANGEMENTS

Although available flowers were not the same in all countries and at all times, and though many of the flowers that we cultivate today were unheard of in times past, there is no reason to limit ourselves for the purpose of historical perfection.

When making a fresh flower arrangement, we can use whatever is in season, choosing those flowers that will best complement in color and form the container we are using and the room in which the arrangement is to be placed. As the gardener-arranger will be limited to whatever is blossoming in his particular climate, flowers of suitable color and form should be planted. The relationship of the plant to the container is, next to harmony with the furnishings and space around it, the most important aspect of period flower arranging.

Decide whether the room is formal or informal, for this will govern the choice of a container, which will in turn influence the materials chosen for the arrangement. While it was once thought that certain flowers were "formal" or "informal," this is not necessarily true for period arranging. Many of our cultivated flowers are derived from field flowers, and in past centuries those blossoms that today are thought of as informal were often all that were available. Formality often may be obtained through the shape of the arrangement rather than from the materials that go into it.

BASIC MECHANICS FOR FRESH FLOWER ARRANGING

There are basic aids for modern flower arrangements and these may be used in the period pieces if they help create the proper effect.

It is helpful to have on hand pinholders of various shapes and sizes. These are heavy metal disks with protruding nails used to anchor flowers to the bottom of the container and to hold the flowers upright. Pinholders are usually necessary when you are using a shallow dish. A small ball of florist's clay placed on the bottom of the pinholder will attach the holder firmly to the container. Florist's wire can be used to tie several blossoms together and create the illusion of one large flower, or to strengthen and support more fragile stems. When grouping flowers in this manner, be certain that all stems will reach the water. Do not fasten the wire too tightly or the flowers will not absorb the water. Remove all foliage from the portion of the stems to be immersed.

BASIC MECHANICS FOR DRIED AND ARTIFICIAL FLOWERS

When arranging plastic or any other type of artificial flower with wired stems, an essential tool is a medium-sized wire cutter. The cutter must be strong enough to cut through the heavy wire stems often found on good-quality artificial flowers and foliage.

Another tool necessary for arranging plastic flowers is a pair of scissors for trimming leaves or petals. Florist's wire is useful for tying flower stems together, or for adding an extra length to a flower stem that is too short.

To achieve a natural look in plastic flower bouquets, thrust the flower stems into a styrofoam holder. In making tall arrangements it is usually necessary to anchor plastic flowers which do not arrange themselves as gracefully as do fresh flowers. Once they are firmly anchored, the stiff wire stems can be bent into graceful lines. When making arrangements for tall containers, cut the styrofoam with an ordinary kitchen knife to fit the bottom of the container as closely as possible and then wedge it in tightly with scraps of styrofoam. When working with shallow containers, anchor the styrofoam block or sphere with florist's clay as detailed above. (A two-sided sticking tape can hold the styrofoam in a shallow container, but the florist's clay works as well.)

HOW TO PURCHASE PLASTIC FLOWERS

Plastic flowers are now made so realistically that they can be used on occasion as a substitute for fresh flowers. As a rule, the flowers worth displaying with fine furniture and carefully chosen backgrounds are the most expensive, for they are reproduced as accurately as possible. Botanically perfect plastic flowers, made to careful specifications in Hong Kong, Italy, or France, are a perfect answer for those who wish to have a lasting arrangement without the worry about what is available in the garden or at the florist's. Although still frowned upon by garden club members and veteran flower arrangers, plastic flowers have become accepted by the most particular interior designers. A period room can now be completely decorated with the proper arrangements in the right shape, size, and colors. With permanent flowers, a room need not be without floral decoration for nine months of the year, looking bare and unfinished.

Plastic flowers have other advantages. They are nonallergenic and washable, and an arrangement will remain as intended indefinitely. Also, when plastic flowers are arranged in an antique container, it need not be one that will hold water. A cracked or chipped container may be used and

*This arrangement of dried material in shades of brown
is brightened by the use of Japanese container with
multicolored allover design*

the fault camouflaged by the arrangement. Damaged antique
dishes, teapots, cups, and vases that one might never be able
to own in mint condition may be purchased at reasonable
prices.

Still another advantage of artificial flowers and foliage is
that one is more likely to make the effort necessary to make
complicated arrangements suitable for decorative periods if
they are not to be disposed of in a day or a week. There are

13

many places in a room where an arrangement would bring color and texture to the decor, and a lasting flower bouquet can be planned ahead as part of the total room decoration.

The living topiary, typical of the formal gardens of Louis XIV, requires a long growing time and a difficult training procedure. It is impractical as an indoor house plant. Copies using cut foliage require too much of the flower arranger's time and patience for the few days that the flower arrangement can be enjoyed before it wilts. A topiary tree made from plastic foliage on a base of styrofoam will last indefinitely.

The art of flower arranging may be a more pleasurable one, therefore, if lasting flowers are used. Now that plastic

Holders for arranging flowers in vases were made in the late eighteenth century in England. This one of black basalt is particularly graceful when used alone with bunches of starflowers

The bouquet style of arranging flowers was used consistently
before this century. This arrangement of pink artificial
camellias and dried baby's-breath is in a luster bowl

flowers, fruit, and foliage are made so perfectly that they
must be touched in order for one to establish whether they
are real or artificial, these materials may be used anywhere to
enchance the ambience of a room.

DRIED PLANT MATERIAL

Because dried flowers and other dried, natural materials have
become so popular as room decorations, there is a greater
variety from which to choose than ever before. Although
many of the conventional dried flowers and foliage are
highly suitable for the Early American or Victorian periods,
others now on the market may be used for arrangements for
many other periods. Some of the sturdier materials, formerly
available only in drab natural colors, are now dyed or

sprayed so that they are appealing to those who desire color as well as texture and form for their arrangements. One can buy blue thistle imported from Italy, eranthis plumes in a variety of colors, wheat dyed any hue, or bunches of tiny starflowers dyed nearly any color of the rainbow. These certainly make more interesting arrangements than the somber winter bouquets which used to sit on top of the family Victrola.

Dried material is most in abundance at florists' shops and boutiques in the fall. This is the time to stock up, for the bunches of green starflowers that might be just what you will want for an arrangement in a particular bowl in the coming winter might not be available later in the season. Even plastic flowers are somewhat seasonal. A florist's advertisement for "New spring flowers just arrived" may apply as well to plastic flowers as to fresh ones.

There are so many good sources that give directions for drying flowers that this subject will not be discussed here. For those interested in drying their own garden flowers and foliage, there are many interesting possibilities for arrangement materials. Many flowers not conventionally used for dried bouquets are nevertheless interesting when dried and used for period arrangements.

RESTORING ANTIQUE CONTAINERS

Most of us interested enough in one particular style of decoration to have furnished a room or an entire home in it do not mind further investment in antique accessories. They are always a good investment for the future, and the beauty of these articles will be enchanced by their use with flowers, fruit, or foliage.

With today's renewed interest in antiques, the flower arranger will find it increasingly difficult to purchase for small sums perfect examples of old pottery, porcelain, pewter, and silver to use as containers. Ordinarily, no one would advise buying broken, cracked, or chipped antiques, but many of these articles are ideal for the flower arranger. If an old container is not too badly damaged, often it can be restored to be used as a holder for an arrangement. Flaws can be hidden with flowers or foliage and frequently a container that cannot be used to hold fresh flowers because it will not hold water is ideal for artificial or dried bouquets.

There are certain types of damage which do not detract too much from the value of small decorative antiques. For example, old ironstone pottery that one might otherwise hesitate to purchase because this type of ware often has brown stains or "time cracks" can usually be cleaned and the appearance improved by soaking it for several days in a strong solution of chlorine bleach. This will not damage the glaze or decoration of a dish, and the stains will usually either disappear or fade considerably. A really good antique dish that is chipped or badly cracked should be taken to a professional workman who specializes in antique china and pottery. If a dish is not too valuable and it not going to be used with water, Elmer's Glue-All will hold it together well enough for it to be used as a decorative container. A new product, Dow Corning Glass and Ceramic Adhesive, is now available for repairing china and pottery; and it is both waterproof and heatproof.

If an appealing antique glass vase has a chipped top, buy it and have the rim ground down. Be sure that the chips are not too deep or the grinding will impair the shape of the piece and it will no longer be graceful and in good proportion. On the other hand, do not buy glassware that is badly cracked, because it is expensive to have it repaired professionally, and sometimes the ride home will cause enough of a jolt for the crack to become a break. In any case, cracks show badly in glass.

There are commercial preparations especially made for polishing brass, copper, and pewter. If a "find" is a particularly good piece, it may be cleaned professionally and possibly lacquered, so that when it is used for flowers the arrangement need not be disturbed for frequent polishing.

Victorian picture frames with gold leaf inserts, useful for dried pressed arrangements, are difficult to find in mint condition; they can be repaired if the gold leaf is merely scaling or chipped, or if the wood is nicked or scratched. Small dents or scratches in the wood can be repaired with wax crayon sticks which come in a variety of wood tones. Often, simply a good rubbing with paste wax will restore the frame to usable condition. The gold leaf may be filled in with "Treasure Gold," a semidry paint that is easy to apply with the fingertip or a small brush. "Treasure Gold" can be used to repair the finish on anything with a gold or bronze plating, and it can be used for antiquing or highlighting other finishes with gold. It is available in a variety of metallic shades and in gold leaf. Follow the directions that come with the jar of paint.

Most antique wooden boxes can be refinished or repaired, but unless the box is in really poor condition a good coat of paste wax will usually remove dirt and restore the wood grain without taking away the desirable "old look." To restore the patina, use a little paste wax and a lot of elbow grease.

3

Historical Periods
in Decoration

What today is meant by period decoration? How can one recognize the various periods and their furnishings?

Furniture, wall papers, and fabrics have certain distinguishing characteristics that reflect the period in question and the country of origin. Small accessories also have identifiable styles.'In furniture, these characteristics find their expression in a combination of overall shape or line and in harmonious decorative elements such as carving or applied molding, inlay, hardware, painted details, and combinations of these. Usually these stylistic characteristics evolved over a span of years. Occasionally a great designer hastened a trend. Such an artist was Chippendale, whose designs were adapted from a combination of previous furniture patterns, but original in conception and distinctive in design. Others followed the current fashion, copying or adapting it to their tastes. It still takes many years for advanced designs to be accepted widely enough to become a trend or style.

Few periods in the decorative arts have been completely original. The evolution of furniture design can be traced and retraced throughout the past five hundred years; repetition of, and borrowing from, the past have been techniques used since the Renaissance. Usually designs from a former century were combined with current ones, resulting in hybrid fashions that were distinctive in their own way. For example, though the Victorians' penchant for eclecticism revived Gothic, French Baroque, and other elaborate furniture

The Gothic style was revived several times in the history of the decorative arts. This washbowl and pitcher set are from the Victorian period. The arrangement in the bowl uses artificial blue flowers sprayed with paint made to give plastic flowers a pearlized iridescent color

21

styles, it is not too difficult to identify furniture from the Victorian period. The pure, true feeling of each period is evident to the educated and discerning eye, no matter what style the designs were adapted from.

Changes in furniture styles were due to many factors in the development of Western civilization. Trade with China for many years brought Far Eastern arts and crafts into European lives and influenced the Western decorative arts perhaps more than any other single factor. Economy, government, and religion have also strongly inspired the development of the decorative arts. The strong French influence found in the furniture styles of England during the eighteenth century was a result of French artisans having fled to England in search of religious freedom.

Furniture of each country of Europe, although made in one period and one basic style, is interpreted differently. Thus English Gothic styles differ from the Gothic styles of Italy, Flanders, and Germany. The Baroque furniture of Italy differs from that of the same period in France.

Periods in the decorative arts run their course of rise, climax, and decline. Often new styles were created when a new ruler came on the scene, even though change had begun earlier. During the rule of Louis XIV, French decorative arts depended entirely on the whim of the King and his court. Court furniture was designed and made expressly for the King's use. Although the French styles were the ones most frequently copied by nobles during the late seventeenth and eighteenth centuries, royal patronage bankrupted the treasury and helped eventually to create the proper climate for revolution. Once Napoleon had seized power, designers

Blue and white transfer-printed gravy boat of the nineteenth century holds an arrangement of blue and white flowers

set about creating a new style of furniture. Thus each important period in French furniture design bears the name of the ruler or political regime then in power. Royal patronage, while it lasted, was responsible for some of the finest furniture ever made.

It is easy to identify most period furniture, but we also come upon furniture that is obviously old but whose dominant characteristics are of more than one period. Often there is nothing about it that puts it into a distinct category. We must remember that the English cabinetmakers did not one

*In the early twentieth century Japanese motifs were copied
in America and England. This arrangement of starflowers
is in an English bone china bowl decorated with Japanese motifs*

day stop making Jacobean furniture and decide to make everything in the style of William and Mary. Most of the major changes in styles of furniture evolved over a long period of time, and therefore we find many transitional pieces that have characteristics of two periods.

Except when speaking of furniture mass-produced in the Victorian period, reference to identifying characteristics of chairs or tables is to the very best examples of each period, and to the shape, decoration, wood, hardware, and workmanship that epitomize the best of a style. Until fairly late in the history of the decorative arts, most furniture was made for the nobility. Peasants made do with the simplest articles: a bench, a box, a bed, and perhaps a table. In the eighteenth century the lower classes sometimes copied articles made for the aristocracy, and as a middle class developed in different parts of Europe, a country style of furniture adapted from contemporary fashions began to be made in quantity. Therefore, although a provincial Queen Anne table might be as graceful as those seen today in museums, the quality of the workmanship and the wood nevertheless would set it apart from the finest examples of that period.

Characteristics that help to identify furniture with the period in which it belongs (and often, its country of origin) are the metal and form of the hardware, turning or lack of it on stretchers and legs of tables and chairs, the inlay or marquetry, the paint, and other details. The good designs were copied or adapted both at home and in other countries, but usually the origin is apparent to the trained eye. It is not our purpose here to stress the difference between genuine period furniture and fakes or reproductions, but simply to give some general feeling of each important decorative period so that the flower arrangements the reader makes will convey the characteristics of those periods.

Descriptions of the three general classifications of the decorative arts—Baroque, Rococo, and Classic—might be enough of a guide for the adept flower show contestant, but the home decorator, in order to make the proper flower arrangement for a particular style of furniture, should have further guidelines. Even in an eclectic room in which a number of periods are harmoniously combined, the arranger will find that working within the confines of a particular period will result in more pleasing compositions. Although a Chippendale sideboard is now used in the same room as a Queen Anne table, each piece of furniture should display the small decorative antiques of its own period, and the flower arrangements should be similarly compatible. A well-made flower arrangement in a container of the same period as the

The Victorians looked back on all the previous decorative periods and adapted styles from all of them. This cherub is a bronzed toothpick holder made in Victorian times in a French antique style. The flowers are miniature silk roses and forget-me-nots

furniture on which it is to be placed often helps to coordinate a room furnished in eclectic style. The following chapters, although not able to give a complete picture of furniture for each period, should help in identifying furniture of the past and also give one a feeling for the type of flower arrangement that will suit a particular style of interior decoration.

4

The Gothic Period

Flowers have been a means of expression in art, religion, and decoration since the beginning of civilization. Ancient Egyptians grew and used flowers for their beauty and fragrance, as gifts to the gods, and for funeral offerings. Early tomb paintings in Egypt record offerings of bowls of flowers, and ancient embroideries of flowers remind us of their importance to the civilizations of the past.

For the ancient Greeks, wreaths and garlands were symbols of allegiance, and special wreaths using a particular leaf or flower, such as the laurel wreath, depicted a particular honor. As in many other forms of ancient art, flowers became not only a symbolic part of religious life in many early societies, but a decoration for the home as well. The ancient Romans used flowers for banquet decorations, and early Roman mosaics record how flowers were arranged in containers for the home.

On the European continent the first period of interior design that is significant in regard to flower arrangement is the Gothic period. In architecture it reached its peak in France and spread also into England, Italy, and Germany. France seems to have exercised the strongest influence, not only on architecture but also on room design and furniture during the Gothic times.

Gothic furniture took its design mainly from ecclestiastical buildings, and this architectual style, with its arches and decorated geometrical forms, dominated furniture design on the Continent for three centuries. Presently existing furniture of the late fifteenth century and early sixteenth century is often church furniture. From the point of view of the

Hammered bronze ewer is typical of containers of the Persian influence in the Gothic period. The flowers used are cosmos and asters. The butterfly is a real one, treated to preserve it

Arrangement of hydrangeas, geraniums, and Lunaria in Gothic-style pitcher registered by Job Meigh in 1842. This "Minster jug," which is encircled with Gothic arches containing figures of the apostles in relief, has been called the finest example of Victorian Gothic revival

decorator and flower arranger, this period is interesting, and the Gothic influences are important to recognize because they have been utilized by various furniture designers and architects. The style was revived and copied or adapted in the eighteenth century and more widely during the nineteenth century. Especially in England, under Queen Victoria, the Gothic style flourished, and these revival pieces are now eagerly sought by collectors.

Because Gothic architectural style has been used almost continuously for church buildings, the flower arranger often has the opportunity to make bouquets that are in keeping with Gothic style architecture.

Gothic "jewelled" chalice was made by spraying a modern
milk glass goblet with gold paint and glueing make-believe
rubies and emeralds on the sides and foot. Arrangement of red
tearoses and green fern creates an unusual Christmas decoration

Shades of green in the sedum and snakegrass give a subtle color
interest to arrangement made in a Gothic-style
smear-glaze pitcher

DECORATIVE ACCESSORIES FOR THE GOTHIC PERIOD

Bronze, brass, and porcelain vases and ewers were used in the Gothic period. These articles were brought to the European continent from Persia in the fifteenth century by Venetian merchants, and they appear in paintings of that century. Many of these *objets d'art* are made in the Near East today, in styles similar to those that appear in secular paintings of the sixteenth century. The Venetian merchants who bought from Persia also traded with Northern Europe, and the decorative accessories of that period were often of Oriental origin.

FLOWER ARRANGEMENTS FOR THE GOTHIC PERIOD

Arrangements of soft colors (perhaps including irises, roses, tulips, and violets, with green foliage) reflect the Persian influence that was strongly felt during the Gothic period.

For use with Gothic revival furniture of the nineteenth century, an arrangement of flowers in a carved wooden box is appropriate.

Large, loose, bouquet-type arrangements in gold-sprayed containers may be used for altars and other arrangements in churches.

5

The Renaissance and the Italian Influence in Decoration

     The dawn of the Renaissance in the early fifteenth century marks the beginning of Italian influence on all the arts of Western culture. Although comparatively little furniture was used in the great rooms of that period, there are examples of *cassoni* and *credenze* that are designed in simple, restrained, classic style. A *cassone* is a chest or large box with its decoration carved, painted, or inlaid—or combinations of these may be used. A *credenza* is a kind of low sideboard, with doors, drawers.

  Restrained classical design was typical of all the arts of the early Renaissance, but by the seventeenth century the austerity had disappeared, and the ornate, lavish, dramatic Baroque style evolved. Its later aspect is more cosmopolitan due to the influence of the French, Spanish, and Dutch.

  Italian furniture in the fifteenth and sixteenth centuries was always made of walnut. Many of the earlier pieces were painted, and raised gesso ornaments were lavishly used, often gilded. These methods of decorating furniture waned toward the start of the Baroque period when lavish heavy carving became the main decoration.

By the late seventeenth century, French, Dutch, and English styles became more prominent and Italian leadership in furniture design declined as Italy's wealth and commerce declined. Craftsmanship suffered as the best artisans moved to France, Germany, and England. Although the classic forms of the Renaissance were totally Italian in their origin, their interpretation by these expatriates resulted in a new style of decorating that became traditionally French.

Renaissance style candlestick is displayed with an arrangement made in a wicker basket sprayed gray to resemble a pottery bowl of the period

*Bright orange and yellow chrysanthemums in an
Italian drug jar* (JAR, COURTESY OF MARIE WHITNEY ANTIQUES)

In the sixteenth century there was a period in England when the Italian influence on the decorative arts was strong. Under Henry VIII, Italian artisans and their fabrics, furniture, and decorative ornaments were brought to England to help give identity to the newly established Church of England. Thus there was a new style in England that was called Tudor but was really Italian.

"Italian Provincial" and "Mediterranean" are terms often used to describe some of today's furniture based on Italian designs. Although most of this furniture has little to do with any furniture ever made in Italy, there are certain Italian characteristics apparent in some of the better designs. To-

34

New Italian bread basket was sprayed gold, placed on wood
base, and filled with a symmetrical arrangement of artificial
blue and orange daisies

Fleur-de-lis design is a Venetian adaptation of a Renaissance
motif. This arrangement of marigolds, roses, and foliage was
made to carry out design on Italian container

*For this arrangement the inspiration came from a della Robbia
ceramic. Scale is important in relating the urn to the materials
used. The marble base gives arrangement the height it needs*

day's marble table tops show the Italian influence, as does
some of the geometric paneling on the case furniture. The
use of dark woods, particularly walnut, gives the proper feeling of Italian influence, and the formal design of Renais-
sance-style chairs has been adapted for modern seating.

DECORATIVE ACCESSORIES AND FLOWER
ARRANGEMENTS FOR RENAISSANCE AND
ITALIAN-INFLUENCED FURNITURE

Rich, dark colors in fabrics and dark wood tones call for deep colors in the flower arrangements, and dark red, blue, and green are the colors most often favored. Suitable containers may be of alabaster, wood, heavy silver, pewter, or majolica. Foliage arrangements in dark wood containers are a perfect adjunct to Italian styling in present-day furniture.

Victorian crystal compote resembles Venetian glass when filled with arrangements in della Robbia style (COMPOTES FROM THE COLLECTION OF MR. & MRS. RICHARD N. FRIED)

6

Spanish Influence on Furniture Design

        While there is no furniture in the history of the decorative arts that can be singled out as having originated in Spain, there has always been a strong, masculine vigor in Spanish interpretations of borrowed design. The widespread use of black wrought iron for furniture and small decorative objects is typically Spanish.

        Perhaps the best way to discuss Spanish influence is to pay little attention to the fact that all furniture styles in Spain have been adaptations of foreign styles, and to give more emphasis to those characteristics that are typically Spanish. Motifs brought to Spain by the conquering Moors now have become typically Spanish. These motifs are found on tiles, fabrics, and wallpapers, old and modern. Moorish patterns include stars, geometrical arabesques, and inlaid borders often found in walnut and other woods.

        Early Renaissance furniture design in Spain was adapted from the Italians. Because the Spanish furniture makers were not craftsmen, the workmanship on much of the old Spanish furniture is far inferior to similar designs made in other countries. Often this poor craftsmanship was covered over with paint. Metal ornaments and wrought iron stretchers were used from a very early period. Wrought iron ornamentation was used in abundance on houses, also.

In the settlements in the American hemisphere, a Spanish Colonial style developed that has somewhat influenced furniture and decorating approaches in many sections of the world and particularly in certain areas of the United States. "Mission" furniture, which was made in the United States

Stoneware jug holds bright arrangement of yellow,
orange, and magenta strawflowers

*Wrought iron stand with arrangement of miniature
plastic vegetables in natural, bright colors*

at the beginning of the twentieth century, was an adaptation
of the furniture of the early Spanish missions in the American southwest. This dark oak furniture, heavy, plain, and
functional, is currently being sought by collectors. Spanish
peasant furniture evolved into a style in Mexico that has

great popularity in the American southwest and elsewhere; this is brightly painted and features peasant designs.

FLOWER ARRANGEMENTS FOR SPANISH-STYLE DECORATION

Perhaps the area of the decorative arts where the Spanish influence can be the most interesting is in the field of flower arranging. The somber dark woods and black ironwork of typical Spanish furniture, which is usually placed against

Majolica jug with cobalt blue, gray, and brown glaze holds arrangement of blue-dyed thistles and other dried materials in grays and shades of brown

*Gaily decorated Mexican pottery holds bouquet
of bright Mexican paper flowers*

light or white walls, call for bright colors in the flower arrangements. Bright primary hues are usually identified with Spanish decoration, and the possibilities for Spanish-style flower arrangements are exciting and virtually unlimited.

Mexican paper flowers, brightly colored hemp flowers, and dried strawflowers, as well as fresh garden flowers in brilliant colors, are particularly appropriate for Spanish peasant decoration. Simple pottery, wrought iron containers, and handcrafted baskets are all suitable for this type of arrangement.

*Arrangement of hens-and-chicks with manzanita branch
in a Zuñi Indian pottery dish harmonizes with Mission
furniture styles, also simple modern furniture*

7

The Elizabethan and Jacobean Periods

The English Renaissance, which began under the Tudors, continued until the middle of the seventeenth century. Characteristic furnishings were a combination of Italian, Germanic, French, and Flemish designs and details. From this combination evolved in the second half of the sixteenth century the style which we designate today as Jacobean. Until Tudor times English decorative arts did not favor movable furniture, and what little there was of it, the nobility owned. The melon-bulb leg, so massive in Elizabethan times, became lighter in the Jacobean versions. Carving, so bold and exuberant in Tudor days, became flatter and more refined. Large, heavily-carved chests, which were used for storage and often for seating, were typical of this period. Borders of intertwined circles, diamond-shaped carvings and moldings, turned legs, and applied carved panels adorned oak chests and tables. Much Flemish cabinet work was imported.

Chairs of the Jacobean period had high backs, turned, straight legs, and wooden or upholstered seats, although the Italian X-chair with crossed legs forming an X was common, too. Flemish-derived chairs had cane seats. This chair design, or derivations of it, has been revived periodically and is once again in favor with interior designers.

The French influence in English furniture design became

Early pottery tankard arranged with artificial snowberries and miniature lemons in a small table arrangement

Delft vase with Baroque arrangement of various brightly colored flowers and green ferns (VASE, COURTESY OF MARIE WHITNEY ANTIQUES)

decidedly more obvious as many French artisans fled to England in search of religous freedom after the Edict of Nantes was revoked in 1685. The French influence was felt almost immediately, and the cabriole leg was seen in English furniture for the first time. Curves were more common now than on the earlier, more angular furniture. By the close of the seventeenth century, furniture, previously found only in homes of the nobility, was being made on a smaller scale for homes of the middle classes—but it was still large by modern-day standards.

Carved motifs used on Jacobean furniture were in the forms of flowers, shells, foliage, and fruit. In the homes of the nobility, heraldic designs were frequent decorations on walls and furniture. Oak was the prevailing wood for furniture.

This was also the early period of development in the American colonies, and the Jacobean style appears in our early imported furniture and in American copies and adaptations.

DECORATIVE ACCESSORIES FOR THE JACOBEAN PERIOD

After the British East India Company was incorporated in 1600, goods from China, India, and the Middle East increasingly were imported by England. Oriental rugs were used in

Small pewter tankard arranged with spring garden flowers
(TANKARD, COURTESY OF MARIE WHITNEY ANTIQUES)

large rooms of the wealthy, and embroideries and elaborate fabrics of silk and damask were used for wall hangings. Chintz and linen were also used as wall coverings. Many of the domestic fabrics had Oriental motifs, and crewel embroidery was widely used.

During this period of trade with China, porcelain was introduced, and the drinking of tea, chocolate, and coffee spread the popularity of fine china teacups throughout a country which heretofore had used only crude pottery, pewter, and woodenware for eating and drinking utensils. Porcelain became a highly prized commodity, and the influence of Chinese porcelain motifs in the decorative arts of the Western world was to be felt for centuries to come. Much of the English china made today reproduces the shapes and designs of Chinese porcelain. It is interesting to note that the Chinese porcelain most favored by the English during the Jacobean period was the elaborately decorated ware, while Chinese vases of monochromatic glazes or with simple blue and white decoration appealed to the French.

FLOWER ARRANGEMENTS FOR THE JACOBEAN PERIOD

Flower arrangements for the Jacobean period should be informal, made in large and showy bouquets. Although the fabrics of that period are what we would consider formal today, the oak furniture was less refined. Pewter tankards and pitchers are excellent containers for arrangements of spring flowers in full bouquets that dominate the spot for which they are made. Foliage arrangements in carved oak boxes will suit

Large pewter jug holds only six well-made artificial tulips and fern. This tall arrangement can be used on a Jacobean sideboard or in another spot where height is welcome

Jacobean decoration very well; simple arrangements of fall foliage in elaborate Chinese-style vases and bowls are also appropriate.

Small arrangements of flower bouquets in old Chinese teapots or teacups may be used as accessories for a Jacobean setting. Because there was little interest in horticulture in this period in England, field flowers should predominate. Delft vases, which are still reproduced, are good containers for informal arrangements, and woodenware of simple design is a fine foil for arrangements of fruit or vegetables.

8

The William and Mary Period

Between the Jacobean and Queen Anne periods there was a confusion of influences on English decoration. King William had brought Continental tastes to the British throne with him, and eventually Italian, Flemish, and French styles blended into a style that was most strongly inspired by Dutch influences.

The period of William and Mary began about 1700 in England and about 1720 in America. The style was important in America, for the styles of English furniture designers and cabinetmakers were invariably adapted in the Colonies. As the economy of the Colonies burgeoned at the beginning of the eighteenth century, rooms became larger and the grand style and elegance of William and Mary furnishings were eagerly embraced and easily adapted.

At the same time, English trade with the East had become even more important to the British economy. Queen Mary collected china and porcelain. By example, she intro-

Chinese teapot holds arrangement of blue plastic roses

duced her subjects also to fine needlework and other refinements of the home. Wood paneling became popular, and carved ornamentation was used around doors and windows. Architecture and furnishings became more elaborate as some of the large furniture was scaled to smaller proportions, while other usually small pieces were enlarged in scale; on the whole, scale became more important, producing a more harmonious relationship between architecture and home furnishings.

In furniture, the curved line became more dominant,

Baroque arrangement in alabaster urn utilizes many varieties
of peach-colored flowers sprayed with "pearlized" paint.
The urn is placed on a carved alabaster stand

showing the French influence that had begun to refine and
change the style of the bulky, carved Jacobean furniture.
More thought was given to the form and finish of furniture
rather than to its embellishment. The grain and color of the
wood became more important to furniture design, and walnut rather than oak was now the favored wood. Toward the
end of the seventeenth century, upholstered and padded
seats and backs, covered with needlework, were used on
chairs. Lacquered and marquetry-embellished furniture was
popular; the marquetry, often copied from Dutch styles, was
carefully matched and intricate.

*Miniature table arrangement of artificial sedum and
begonia leaves in brass container on teak stand*

SMALL DECORATIVE ANTIQUES FOR THE WILLIAM AND MARY PERIOD

Because trade with the Orient was so important during the William and Mary period, and because porcelain and lacquer work from China were available to decorate the fine homes of England and America, the Chinese influence was in ascendance in the early eighteenth century.

Baroque arrangement is composed of summer garden flowers in a Chinese Export bowl on a teakwood stand (BOWL, COURTESY OF MARIE WHITNEY ANTIQUES)

*Pewter urn of the period holds dried arrangement using
statice, fern seed pods, and cattails* (URN, COURTESY
OF MARIE WHITNEY ANTIQUES)

The Chinese had not decorated their vases heavily
enough to suit English tastes, and British workmen added
their own ornamentation: Baroque was still the most popular
design element in the decorated porcelain of England. Delft
from Holland was still popular, and English copies of the
blue-and-white ware were made toward the end of the seventeenth century. English silver of this period is elaborately
decorated, and brasses and pewter were more elaborate than
they had been previously. Tapestries and embroideries were

still used in decoration, as were linen and chintz, but silk grew in popularity as a decorative fabric.

FLOWER ARRANGEMENTS FOR THE WILLIAM AND MARY PERIOD

Flowers for use with William and Mary furniture can be elaborately arranged. The Baroque effect of a bouquet of large-size flowers in an elaborately decorated container can convey the feeling of the period very well. The containers for this period are ornate, and silver, pewter, and brass are appropriate. The William and Mary period was one of grandeur in decorating and calls for massive flower arrangements on a scale with the furniture. However, when a table arrangement is needed, small porcelain bowls, decorated silver pitchers, and Chinese teapots are quite in keeping with the style of the period if the flowers are arranged in the Baroque manner. Do not employ monochromatic schemes for arrangements, but use many kinds and colors of flowers in bouquets.

9

Early American Decoration

Colonists coming to America
in the seventeenth century brought with them whatever they
could in the way of household effects. The first settlers who
came to New England were not members of the aristocracy
but Puritans in search of religious freedom. They had an
austere outlook on life and they frowned on fashion. Ac-
cordingly, their oaken furniture was mostly of the cruder
Elizabethan styles. Included were Bible boxes, trestle tables,
and court cupboards. Whatever furniture could not be
shipped across the Atlantic was made as soon as possible in
the Colonies, and in exactly the same style. It is difficult,
therefore, to be certain whether the pieces of furniture that
have survived this earliest period were made in England or
America.

On the other hand, the Jacobean style, which was favored
by the aristocracy, was brought first to Virginia by the Royal-
ists, who had been accustomed to better things than had the
New England settlers, and the Virginian colonists continued
to import the latest styles from their mother country. As

Virginia prospered, their homes continued to reflect the latest architectural styles of England.

American craftsmen were well established by the end of the seventeenth century, and artisans from Holland, Sweden, England, and France also settled in various areas of the Colonies, making furniture that reflected their heritage. In the New York area, Chinese and Spanish motifs were

Gloriosa daisies are the accent flower of this informal
garden bouquet in an old wooden butter tub

*Fake or real vegetables in an old wooden salad bowl make
an informal centerpiece for a country kitchen*

introduced by Dutch settlers. The Chinese influence resulted from the trade the Netherlands had carried on with
the Far East, and the Spanish influence had been impressed
upon the Dutch when Spain occupied the Netherlands.
Many Swedes settling in the Hudson Valley worked with
the Dutch artisans, adding still another influence to furniture making and decoration.

Both Swedish and Dutch influences were strongly felt in
the early furniture of Pennsylvania. After the arrival of
William Penn, settlers came from all over Europe to the new
territory he had established, but the furniture design that we

*Joe-Pye-weed and other field flowers in an early
handmade tole dipper*

now call Pennsylvania Dutch is primarily a combination of
early Dutch, Swedish, and German influences. This is a type
of country furniture that was brought over by the early
settlers, especially the Germans, who came to the new continent at Penn's invitation. It found favor among many
residents and was copied and adapted for many years.

Pennsylvania Dutch furniture is therefore similar to several kinds of European peasant furniture. Perhaps most
typical of items in this category is the gaily painted dower
chest, which is often copied. This furniture was usually
made of pine and belongs in the category of American coun-

try furniture, but some of the most refined and sophisticated furniture of early America was made in the Pennsylvania area.

As English furniture styles developed, Pennsylvania artisans of the eighteenth century copied and adapted the latest English styles. The first American Windsor chair was made in Philadelphia about 1725, a bit later than the Windsor chairs of England, which originated near Windsor Castle. Variations of Chippendale's sophisticated designs were also made in Philadelphia. While most American styles were derivations of French and English designs, often the proportions were altered and carving patterns were changed, which gave some of the eighteenth-century American furniture a distinctive look.

There are certain articles of furniture, familiar to most Americans, that developed as a sort of national style in the eighteenth century. After the Windsor chair, which was brought to its finest development in America, came the Boston rocker and certain ladder-back chairs. The decorated Hitchcock chair, which appeared in the early nineteenth century, was a product of Connecticut. It is a familiar article of furniture to most Americans simply because so many were produced. Parts were made at the Hitchcock factory and shipped all over America, where the chairs were assembled in dozens of local factories. Many of these chairs, although actually Early Victorian, are thought of today as "Early American."

The reproduction of Early American furniture has evolved in this century into a blend of styles that often has little to do with authentic early furniture. However, it is a

Large handblown green glass demijohn holds bright arrangement of willow branches, mountain ash berries, and marigolds

distinctly American form of home decoration that is extremely popular today, particularly in the New England area. Made of pine, maple, or cherry wood, this furniture is informal, easy to care for, and adaptable to today's methods of mass production. Although a combination of many styles, it is the one typically American design in home decoration.

It blends well both with reproductions of Colonial accessories and with authentic American antiques of the early period.

This evolved Colonial style might be termed "American country furniture." It includes copies of candle stands, small tables, and other articles of furniture that were typical country interpretations of the English formal furniture of the early period. Often a French influence can be detected as well.

SMALL DECORATIVE ACCESSORIES FOR THE COLONIAL PERIOD

The small decorative accessories of seventeenth-century America were the same as for each comparable decorative period in England, as they were either imported or copied in the Colonies. Wallpapers, chinaware, and other articles used to furnish the homes of the wealthier settlers were quite formal. The more typical American accessories are those country-style antiques which were used primarily for utilitarian purposes and were handmade, usually for local sale, by American artisans.

Old stoneware, woodenware, pewter, and tinware are among the earliest of American-made antique accessories. Since most of the very early pieces of this type are now to be found only in museums, it is fortunate for the collector and flower arranger that styles of this type of ware did not change much until well into the eighteenth century. These later pieces of utilitarian ware can still be picked up at country auctions and found in many antique shops that specialize in Early-Americana. Because most of these country antiques were made to be used mainly for food preparation or serving, the lines were simple, there was little or no decoration, and the styles were often rather primitive. The textures of the materials and the simple shapes are ideal for flower containers for an informal setting.

By the time the colonists came to America in the seventeenth century, pottery of several varieties was being made in England. Although some of this pottery was brought by the settlers, it was not long before native pottery was being made and sold throughout the colonies. Because of its fragility, very little of this pre-Revolutionary pottery exists today, but later examples of plates, mugs, and other utilitarian pottery can still be found. Some of the early nineteenth-century ironstone imported from England, as well as American salt-glaze stoneware and redware, turn up occasionally in shops and are excellent companion pieces for Early American decoration. Also, craftsmen are now reproducing some old styles by hand.

Old box in its original painted blue finish holds arrangement of miniature plastic vegetables

Lunaria and Japanese lanterns in container with
painted Pennsylvania Dutch design

Other accessories for floral displays are old wooden bowls,
spice racks, spice-drawer cupboards, knife trays, pipe boxes,
old scales, small coffee grinders, handmade baskets, and
primitive pots and pans made of copper, brass, and iron.
Most of these items are not very decorative in themselves,
but they are enhanced by the addition of flowers. Pewter, a
material which dates back to colonial times in America, is
appropriate both for flower containers and for small decorative accessories accompanying the arrangements. Very old
pewter is likely to be found only in museums, or at premium

Bright yellow strawflowers and statice in a pail with painted Pennsylvania Dutch decoration which enjoys perennial popularity

prices, but good authentic reproductions are available to us today. Most of the other accessories for Early American decoration are also available in reproductions, and as authentic antiques become more and more scarce, most of us will have to settle for these.

FLOWER ARRANGEMENTS FOR THE COLONIAL PERIOD

Certainly the original New England colonists, practical, puritanical, and hard-working as they were, brought bunches of wild flowers indoors to brighten their homes. In addition, ropes of dried onions and garlic, as well as bouquets of herbs hanging over fireplaces to dry, were a practical form of decoration.

Journals tell us that soon after the Colonies were settled

*Dry arrangement in a Bennington pottery soap dish. No flower
holder is needed; the holes in the drain were used for this
arrangement* (DISH FROM THE COLLECTION OF
MR. AND MRS. ROBERT BELFIT)

and the first hard winters over, women began to give more thought to the interiors of their new homes. Although early life in America was somewhat drab, particularly by our standards, it is interesting that the colors we choose to accompany our "modern Early American" furniture are bright and cheerful.

Flower arrangements for the Colonial style of decorating can be informal, with colors of bright red, green, blue, and yellow predominating. Dried materials are appropriate for winter bouquets. Berries, gourds, and other plants symbolic of the harvest look good in low wooden bowls and baskets on a trestle dining table in the fall months. Other dried material such as wheat, cattails, honesty, and thistle are appropriate for taller arrangements.

Because Early American furniture is informal and utilitarian, the flower arrangements that accompany it should also be informal. Flowers, whether fresh, artificial, or dried, should not have a planned look. A simple bouquet loosely arranged in a pewter pitcher or in a tole pan will brighten a pine cupboard or cobbler's bench and make it seem a true picture of its period, whether the furniture is an authentic antique or a reproduction.

10

The Louis XIV Period

At the beginning of the seventeenth century in France, interior decoration was a combination of Italian, German, Swiss, and Flemish influences. As the reign of Louis XIV began, the Italian (or Renaissance) influence still existed, but the French ruler, dedicated to the idea that a great king should influence all of the arts, appointed a state secretary of fine arts, and thereafter, with this impetus, every facet of French art was developed to a high degree.

It was during the reign of Louis XIV that the Versailles palace was begun. The Gobelin tapestry factory became a center for court-appointed artists, weavers, cabinetmakers, and metal workers, who transformed the disparate foreign influences into a positive, elegant French style. The style was robust, symmetrically formal, and sumptuous to the highest degree. Although the cost of maintaining these artists, together with the cost of war and allied extravagances, was to deplete the treasury of France, there is no doubt that Louis XIV was primarily responsible for establishing a truly French national style in the arts.

Realistic topiary is formed on a styrofoam ball base. The material used is plastic spruce (For directions for making topiary see Appendix)

The furniture of the Louis XIV period was massive, with legs modeled after heavily decorated architectural scrolls or animal legs with hoofed feet; eventually the latter became the cabriole leg with its graceful double curve. Gilt bronze mounts decorated the cabinet pieces, while masks, acanthus leaves, and wreaths of laurel and olive were carved into the furniture.

Symmetry of design was typical. The woods were often

painted a strong color, red and green being favored. Marquetry and inlays of bronze, tortoise-shell, brass, ivory, and other materials were much used, and gilded or silvered furniture was also typical of the period.

DECORATIVE ACCESSORIES FOR THE LOUIS XIV PERIOD

Great vases decorated tables and mantels of this period. Bronzes, porcelains, pottery, plaques, and statuary were

The opaline box, old French fan, and white fabric roses create an impression of the opulence of the court of Louis XIV

A boxwood topiary with its focal point of a bright-colored feathered peacock might have come from the gardens of Versailles (For directions for making topiary see Appendix)

made, usually in large proportions, for use with the large-scaled furniture of the time. Small and large Chinese porcelains and Delft pottery were imported; and silk flowers of the type still made today in France became popular.

FLOWER ARRANGEMENTS FOR THE LOUIS XIV PERIOD

Because Louis XIV's influence touched all phases of the decorative arts, royal parks and gardens were developed, and horticulture achieved great importance. Indeed, modern floriculture springs from this period in France. The formal topiary (trimmed evergreen tree) so popular over Europe at this time was typical of the French gardens of the late seventeenth century. Lemon trees and topiaries in pots were also used indoors; and these trees were pruned, trimmed, and trained in restrained beautiful shapes.

As the colors used in textiles were usually strong, bright contrasting bouquets of large proportions are appropriate accessories for rooms of this period. Large flowers and foliage arrangements are suitable. Artificial flowers made of silk will last indefinitely and are in themselves works of art.

All arrangements for the Louis XIV period should be symmetrical, for this is typical of all decoration of this period. Large formal foliage arrangements in the shape of garden topiaries set in garden urns are excellent arrangements also, although they are not completely authentic. These topiaries may be made from plastic foliage on a styrofoam base and used as permanent decorations.

73

11

The Queen Anne Period

A natural evolvement in England from the Jacobean and William and Mary furniture that featured straight lines and heavy turned legs was the Queen Anne style of decoration. This furniture is typefied by curved lines, notably cabriole legs with their graceful double curves, and a lighter overall appearance. It is its elegance, undecorated simplicity, and graceful fluid line that make Queen Anne furniture a popular choice for today's modern homes. The style fits in well with a smaller scale; its graceful proportions are ideal for achieving a formal look in the smaller rooms of houses and apartments today. It is, therefore, a style much used and admired.

During the Queen Anne period, the French influence that had been brought to England and Holland by the French artisans who had fled their own country at the revocation of the Edict of Nantes became dominant, but although the cabriole leg and curved lines of Queen Anne furniture stem from the French, they are, in fact, an English interpretation of the Baroque.

Early brass container with cabriole legs and pad feet holds snake grass, echeveria, and anemones—all realistic but unreal

Windsor chairs, which had originated near Windsor Castle about the time of Anne's accession, became more ornamental during her reign; wings were added to upholstered chairs, and carved decoration was added in the forms of shell designs and claw-and-ball feet. The heavy utilitarian furniture of the past had been so altered as to be almost unrecognizable. The chair expanded into the love seat that was to become a popular style. Heavy ball feet disappeared and were replaced by the Dutch foot or the scrolled bracket foot. Many small and moderate-size pieces became the rule. All furniture was delicately proportioned, and ornamented with restraint and taste. The curved lines and refined, elegantly simple designs are very feminine, yet strong.

Miniature brass coal hod holds real lilies and feverfew from the garden (COAL HOD, COURTESY OF MARIE WHITNEY ANTIQUES)

DECORATIVE ACCESSORIES FOR THE
QUEEN ANNE PERIOD

During this period, trade with China was well established and the influence of Chinese art became strongly felt, lasting throughout the eighteenth century. Shiploads of wallpapers and small decorative accessories were imported from

A brass pitcher contains small plastic blossoms of blue cornflowers and lilies of the valley, realistically made from plastic

China and exported by English merchants to the Colonies. Oriental adaptations of designs from nature (in the forms of flowers, butterflies, and foliage) decorated fabrics, wallpapers, and screens, and the same motifs appeared on porcelains and china. By the middle of the eighteenth century the Chinese influence was so strongly felt that entire rooms were decorated in the Chinese manner. Oriental garden seats with

77

celadon and other glazes, now collector's items, were introduced to the Western world about this time.

The craze for collecting china, both plates and useful pieces as well as *objets d'art* such as figurines, urns, and vases, led to the development of the china cabinet, with shelves to display the collection, and domestic manufacture of china and pottery took on the semblance of Chinese imports.

FLOWER ARRANGEMENTS FOR THE QUEEN ANNE PERIOD

The colors of flowers for arrangements of this period may be soft pastels, with shades of blue, purple, and pink predominating. The arrangements should be symmetrical and not crowded. Round and oval shapes are best suited to Queen Anne style, both in the flowers and the arrangements themselves.

12

The Georgian Period

The reign of Queen Anne was brief—1702 to 1714—so it is apparent that what is today called "Queen Anne" style must have begun at an earlier date and been carried over into a later time. Transition periods are always difficult to pinpoint precisely as to date, but as the Queen Anne period moved into the Georgian period, English design as such was forgotten, and the preference for anything French or Chinese became so widespread that it affected everything decorative, including architecture. Chinese-style summer houses were the latest word in architecture, and fabrics and screens depicting Oriental scenery and family life were used in profusion.

This was the milieu in which Thomas Chippendale began his work as a furniture designer, and the wide acceptance of his work brought the zenith of Oriental influence on Western culture. By the middle of the eighteenth century there was enough wealth in England and America to support trade with the Orient. Most of the pottery and porcelain used by the wealthy at table and for accessories came from China.

This small Oriental bowl holds the first spring pansies

Besides the abundance of Oriental pottery and porcelain imported by England and the Colonies during the Queen Anne and Georgian periods, brasses and pewter were also being made in England and America. Much of it was made in the Oriental style and, to the confusion of today's collectors, these wares were often marked with Chinese-style figures on the underside.

At the beginning of this period in the eighteenth century, however, the pottery industry in England had manifested itself in only a small way. Early salt-glaze stoneware dates from this time in England, and by the middle of the eighteenth century there were many small potteries working in England. Josiah Wedgwood developed his Queen's ware in 1760, and for the first time in English history a typically English tableware was made that the rising middle classes could afford. Heretofore, fine china and porcelain had been available only to the rich, and any china that was made in England was probably a copy of the Chinese style.

Wedgwood's cream-colored earthenware was original in design and non-porous, and because of Josiah Wedgwood's genius in developing a kind of mass production and his improved methods of distribution, this ware soon became available in large enough quantities to satisfy the markets of England, America, and the Continent.

FLOWER ARRANGEMENTS FOR THE GEORGIAN PERIOD

English garden flowers arranged in bouquet-style were still used during the Georgian period, often in Oriental containers. Smaller arrangements were now used in abundance because the furniture was smaller scaled. Footed containers in brass, pewter, or silver, and early English green-glaze pottery are excellent containers for flower arrangements of the Georgian period. Roses are most attractive in bouquet arrangements in formal bowls of this period. Typical dining table arrangements can be made from a combination of fresh and/or artificial fruit.

Oriental-style arrangements employing less material than would have been used for previous periods are appropriate, too. Chrysanthemums or African daisies are good flowers for Georgian arrangements. Because the furniture itself is elegant, though simple and feminine in feeling, elaborate but small arrangements are best.

The craze in England for oriental pottery and porcelain caused enormous amounts of those wares to be imported during the Georgian Period. This Chinese teapot holds a small arrangement of marigolds

The Louis XV Period

After the death of Louis XIV, Philippe d'Orléans acted as Regent from 1715 to 1723. It is mainly due to his influence that the French decorative arts did not decline from the heights reached under Louis XIV but relaxed and modified into softer outlines, employing more ornamentation. French decorative arts became more influential than ever before. Louis XV, brought up in luxury and gaiety, was encouraged in this sophisticated, shallow life by the Royal mistresses, Comtesse Du Barry and the Marquise de Pompadour, the latter being vitally interested in the decorative arts and wielding great power in their development. This period in French art influenced the work of Thomas Sheraton in England, as well as other furniture designers and cabinetmakers in other parts of Europe. From the ornate grandeur and large scale of Louis XIV, furniture and rooms became smaller, more elegant, and quite delicate in feeling.

The contours of Louis XV furniture were elaborately curved; there was little that was linear or straight. The

*Rococo cherubs of Louis XV style in bisque hold lovely
arching arrangement of real red roses and English ivy*
(CONTAINER, COURTESY OF MARIE WHITNEY ANTIQUES)

bombé shape is characteristic of the Louis XV style, the
bulging, curving shape of cabinets and chests echoing the
swelling curves of consoles and tables. The rococo ornamentation that flourished in this era was found on nearly
every piece of furniture. The term *rococo* stems from the
French words meaning rocks (*rocailles*) and shells (*co-
quilles*), and the style so named is balanced, although free-
flowing and irregular. The forms are borrowed freely from
nature—flowers, leaves, rocks, and shells—and worked into
carved and painted ornamentation.

The furniture was small in scale, frequently assymmetri-
cal in design, and for a while the ornamentation was used

with more discretion than heretofore. In the early part of the period, restraint and dignity dictated the use of materials and the proportions. In the later years, structural ornamentation declined into excessive glitter, and ornament for ornament's sake was more the rule, and materials used for making furniture included many kinds of exotic woods. Marquetry was in vogue and employed elaborate, intricate patterns of wood veneers. Inlays of brass, white metal, and ebony were used in fanciful designs. Furniture was often gilded or painted.

The influence of floriculture, begun in the reign of Louis XIV, was now felt in the marquetry and carving which began to appear frequently in elaborate designs of bouquets of flowers, as well as in decorative painted panels on the gilded and painted furniture of the time. Flowers in vases were a frequent motif for inlays. Musical instruments, combined with flowers were another.

SMALL DECORATIVE ACCESSORIES FOR THE LOUIS XV PERIOD

Size was an important factor for accessories in Louis XV rooms as the scale of furniture and dimensions of rooms now were scaled down. The small, feminine French boxes decorated with miniature portraits were created in this period. Chinese *objets d'art* were still popular, but these, too, had become smaller in size. Vases with lacquered flowers and small pots of trees and flowered plants made of porcelain and imported from China were also a decorative feature. Often leaves and flowers were formed of semiprecious stones. Bronze and marble vases were used frequently.

Meissen china figurines, birds, and shrubs were imported

Lasting arrangement in the Rococo style is created from French silk roses and artificial trailing echeveria in pale shades of blue and green. The container is bisque with turquoise-applied enamel and gold (PEDESTAL, COURTESY OF MARIE WHITNEY ANTIQUES)

from Saxony during the reign of Louis XV. Vases lavishly decorated with gold were adorned also with painted scenery and human figures, and decorative stone garden urns were used for planting evergreens intricately trimmed in the newest topiary fashions.

The first French pottery to be made in abundance was produced in St. Cloud, and among the articles recorded were "vases, bowls, and flowerpots." Very little of this ware survives. During the early time of French porcelain production, Chinese motifs were copied and Japanese forms were often used as models; but only toward the end of the reign of Louis XV, when Sèvres porcelains were produced, did a distinctly French china appear. China is still produced at Sèvres today.

Madame de Pompadour was instrumental in establishing the Sèvres manufactory, interesting Louis so much in it that the factory was taken over by the state in 1759 and thereafter concentrated its efforts mainly on producing porcelain for royal use. It was not until his funds were depleted that the extravagant Louis allowed Sèvres porcelain to be made for public purchase. Typical Sèvres porcelain ranges from the regally rococo of Louis XV to the classical revival style of Louis XVI.

While early Sèvres porcelain is now to be found only in museums and private collections, imitations were widely made in the Victorian era. Nineteenth-century ewers, cachepots, and vases are frequently found at auctions and in antique shops, and the shapes and motifs are typically French. Some are too ornate for use except with the most simple flower bouquets, but late Louis XV style shows the transition toward classic motifs which gradually became important as the style merged into that designated as Louis XVI.

FLOWER ARRANGEMENTS FOR THE
LOUIS XV PERIOD

Flower arrangements for the Louis XV period of decorating should be at one and the same time feminine and formal. The natural curving lines of vines are perfect for the rococo style. Many of the rococo-style containers typical of Louis XV will dictate or suggest the shapes of arrangements to be made in them. More care must be given to symmetry and balance than for arrangements of earlier times, and bright colors as well as feminine pastels may be used for the flowers.

White montieth is arranged with daisies and gnaphalium
(MONTIETH FROM THE COLLECTION OF MR. & MRS. RICHARD N. FRIED)

14

French Provincial Style
of Decoration

One sort of country furniture that is more distinctive than most other rural designs and demands further description is French Provincial. It is a style that has become widely accepted today as a separate type of decoration. Although it, like any other national country furniture, is an adaptation or simplification of the refined furniture of a major period of the decorative arts, it has a charm and a restraint that makes it distinctive among the national or peasant styles of decorating.

French country furniture styles were simplified versions of the Louis XV and court (or *château*) furniture, and employed local woods reflecting the areas of France in which the furniture was made. In the seventeenth century in the southern part of France, we find the styles of Louis XIV. This furniture was massive and utilitarian, but frequently employed carvings of flower and foliage forms as decoration. It is interesting that the provincial French artisans of the eighteenth

*Wooden box filled with colorful anemones, white laceflower,
and asparagus fern in a lasting arrangement is placed next to
a lamp base made from old New Orleans balustrade*

century used only a modified version of Louis XV design,
ignoring the style of Louis XVI almost entirely. The modern
versions of French Provincial furniture follow this tradition,
using the graceful cabriole legs and simple carving. The
armoire, a large storage cupboard or closet made of fruitwood
or walnut and possessing gracefully carved paneling, is
typical of French Provincial furniture design.

Because a wealthy bourgeois class grew up in many sections of France during the seventeenth and eighteenth centuries, and because they aped the fashions of the court and the nobility, French Provincial decorative accessories were often of a better quality than those which accompanied other European or provincial furniture. Flocked wallpaper, embroidered and printed fabrics made in France, and fabrics imported from Persia were used for draperies and upholstery. French faïence was the most popular pottery, and pewter was also favored throughout the provinces. The

Rococo pattern on tureen is typical Louis XV design. Fresh garden flowers are daisies, cosmos, asters, and zinnias

curving gadroon edge was typical ornamentation of both pottery and pewter at this time.

True French Provincial furniture reflected the local area from which it originated. Thus the styles from Flanders continued to show their Gothic origin, while furniture made in Alsace in the seventeenth and eighteenth centuries often reflected German or Swiss influences, especially in the use of painted decoration.

The French Provincial styles offered today by furniture manufacturers are feminine but not fussy and can be used with elaborate backgrounds and fabrics. They are usually made of fruitwood or walnut, and they are of the few modern reproductions or adaptations of national styles that consistently remain popular. Most of the French Provincial furniture designs made today are more successful than were

Mustard jar with provincial design holds small informal arrangement of blue pansies and ageratum

*Small arrangement of strawberries is set beside a
strawberry-bordered platter*

Victorian attempts at copying or adapting French antique
designs.

The influence of the eighteenth-century French Provincial style was strong in Canada, where it was brought by
early settlers who continued to make furniture which reflected their native French provinces. French settlers in New
Orleans also left their imprint of the style in the early
architecture and furniture of the southern United States.

SMALL DECORATIVE ACCESSORIES FOR
FRENCH PROVINCIAL DECORATION

Pewter, faïence, pottery, and many other kinds of European
pottery of the period may be used with the French Provincial style. Baskets, wood boxes, carved wood accessories, and
early European kitchenware also may be used for containers.

FLOWER ARRANGEMENTS FOR FRENCH PROVINCIAL DECORATION

The colors used for French Provincial decoration are bright and strong with reds, blues, and greens predominating. Flower arrangements should be informal, and several varieties of flowers may be used together. Bright poppies, anemones, and other flowers indigenous to the fields in the outlying sections of France are appropriate for country-style arrangements. Garden flowers of similar colors and habit of growth can be substituted, of course. Pots of ferns and other feathery foliage in simple containers are also excellent accessories.

Blue jasper pitcher holds arrangement of bright blue and red silk anemones and plastic asparagus fern

15

European Peasant Furniture

Until the eighteenth century, style-setting furniture was designed and made for the court, castles, and manors of England and the Continent. Almost all of this furniture was made on the grand scale by artisans working in the major European cities, for use by the aristocracy and the rich. In the two-class system that prevailed in Europe for many centuries, the peasants lived very simply, and their artisans made furniture that was practical and only somewhat in the style of the time. Regardless of the country, European peasant furniture was basically similar. The necessary furnishings of the peasant cottage—chests, beds, chairs, and tables—were essentially functional pieces of furniture, though in many cases painted or carved decoration was added.

Motifs drawn from religion, superstition, and love were painted in bright colors, and hearts, flowers, and crosses were used both for the painted decorations and in carvings. Animals, some real and some mythical—lions, dragons, and serpents—were used to decorate the furniture.

The major designs and borders were usually geometric, and typical peasant patterns can still be seen in cottage furniture in Europe today. In the history of the decorative arts there have been many times when these early peasant furniture styles have been fashionable, the pieces collected or copied for use by the wealthy. The style is a gay, informal kind of decoration.

As a middle class slowly developed in Europe, those whose fortunes improved wanted decorations similar to the "status" designs of the wealthier classes. These new designs influenced in turn the design of the peasant furniture. There have been few times in fashion when the best styles were

Blue double anemones and asparagus fern are arranged in this pottery pitcher with blue line decoration

*Dried materials include dill seeds, thistle, and wheat
arranged in stoneware butter mold that is rustic in feeling*

not copied or adapted in less formal designs than the originals, and in America, as in Europe, crude copies or adaptations have been made in almost every decorative period since
1700. The crude workmanship, the use of locally available
woods, and the lack of extraneous decoration set this furniture apart from the finest work of each period. The chairs
were sturdy but less graceful. Often the carving was left off
entirely or was more crudely fashioned; straight legs often
replaced the more difficult curves of the cabriole leg; and
when stretchers were used, they were plain and completely
functional. Paint was often used to cover up what was lacking in workmanship; carvings, panels, moldings, and other

Early English creamware cup and saucer with printed decoration of work tools used for gardening in the eighteenth century are a fine foil for a brightly colored but simple arrangement. Yellow marigolds are used with dried baby's-breath sprayed green

designs were simulated on flat surfaces by the artist. Peasant embroideries were used in place of the lavish woven fabrics of the Orient and of European manufacture, as these were so expensive that they were used in only the great houses.

DECORATIVE ACCESSORIES FOR EUROPEAN PEASANT DECORATION

Accessories for the informal peasant furniture should also be informal. Baskets, boxes with simple carving, peasant pottery, and copper, brass, and pewter should be used.

FLOWER ARRANGEMENTS FOR EUROPEAN PEASANT DESIGN

Flowers should be of primary colors, bright and cheerful. Field flowers and branches of flowering shrubs in large bunches can be used. Daisies or black-eyed Susans in huge bunches are particularly effective when placed in old copper pots.

Simple stoneware vase holds a bouquet of wild flowers in an arrangement that complements peasant furniture

16

The Chippendale Style

Thomas Chippendale, a cabinetmaker whose background included a long family tradition in furniture design and manufacturing, was brought by his father (also named Thomas) to England from France, where the older Chippendale had been working. The young Thomas became the most skilled craftsman in the history of English furniture design, but if Chippendale had not, in 1754, published an illustrated catalogue of his designs, thus preserving them for the use of other furniture makers and copiers, the period that is now synonymous with his name might never have been so named. Indeed, had Chippendale himself made all the furniture that now is attributed to him, he would have had to live and work for five hundred years.

The designs in *The Gentleman and Cabinet-Maker's Director* were a combination of several influences. At first the French rococo influence of Louis XV was quite prevalent, but Gothic and Chinese-style furniture became Chippendale's most important contribution. Often applied to

English pottery flower container decorated in oriental style is marked on the underside with Chinese characters, a common practice in Chippendale's time. Job's-tears or other erect flowers are perfect accompaniments

adaptations of the Louis XV and Georgian shapes, the Chinese detail added style and distinction to his solid yet graceful furniture. He was a master of proportion.

The second half of the eighteenth century marked the height of the Chinese influence on both English and French furniture. Carpeting and designs for fabrics were adapted or directly copied from Chinese scrolls and paintings. This was the height of the Western world's trade with China, and it was not until later that Japan opened trade with the West. In many cases the fabric designs combined Chinese patterns with Gothic and French motifs. Art imitated nature in the decorations. Birds, foliage, and all kinds of flowers and trees

Oriental bowl on wood stand is colorful alone and needs only a few silvery lunaria for an attractive miniature table arrangement

were woven in elaborate patterns on magnificent brocades, printed on fabrics, painted on wallpaper, and carved into woodwork.

The Chippendale influence felt in America was usually a simplified version of what had been made in England. Fretwork was used on the backs of chairs, and the cabriole leg and claw-and-ball foot were used extensively. The Americans freely adapted Chippendale's styles and the Chinese decorations found on goods which had been imported from China to England and thence to America. A break from the English influence began as pre-Revolutionary feelings became stronger, and furniture makers of importance arose and began working in America. John Goddard of Newport, Rhode Island, was designing and making furniture that suited colonial needs, and his work was typical of the adaptations of both Queen Anne style and Chippendale designs.

DECORATIVE ACCESSORIES FOR THE
CHIPPENDALE PERIOD

Room accessories of this period are perhaps the most sought-after antiques today. Lacquer boxes, Chinese garden seats, pottery, porcelain—in fact, any of the old Chinese imports—are all in strong demand. Because there were such enormous amounts of porcelain and pottery and other decorative accessories imported from China just before the Revolution, many articles can still be found outside collections, although the number is rapidly dwindling, and the prices mount higher and higher.

It is interesting to note that even as the Western pottery and porcelain makers were copying the Oriental designs pro-

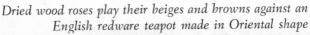

*Dried wood roses play their beiges and browns against an
English redware teapot made in Oriental shape*

fusely, the Chinese were seeking ways to make their pottery and porcelain look more Western. Their decorations for many of the mid- and post-eighteenth century vases, bowls, and dishes were copies of English pottery and porcelain; in many cases the Chinese even attempted to incorporate Occidental human figures into their designs. Their faces, however, betray their Oriental origins. Though the trade continued into the nineteenth century, the second half of the eighteenth century marked the end of the best period of Chinese pottery. Unfortunately, it will probably never be revived again.

Besides the Oriental pottery and procelain, bronze and brass accessories were also typical of this period. Carved teakwood stands and bases were often used under flower vases and containers. English cut glass also became popular during this period. Silver was made both in England and America in designs that simulated Chippendale furniture ornamentation. The pewter of this period was more decorative than it had been previously. Even kitchen utensils, woodenware, and ironstone showed the Chippendale influence and were less crude and better designed than heretofore.

By the time the Chippendale style was at its height in the second half of the eighteenth century, English potters and china makers were producing their wares in abundance and exporting much of it to America. Wedgwood's Queen's ware shapes in the cream-colored clay body still dominated the pottery market, but other potters soon offered important competition. Worcester china was very popular and was exported, also. In Staffordshire, English potters were producing

salt-glaze pottery, much of it using Oriental motifs; majolica, fashioned after early Italian pottery, and the blue-and-
white decorated pottery known as "flow blue" were also
popular. Any of the above are excellent containers which

*Although this majolica compote is nineteenth-century,
its oriental pattern reflects Chippendale period design.
Arrangement for a centerpiece is made of artificial ivy,
anemones, cabbage roses, and Queen Anne's lace*

Small oriental brass dipper is ideal for a coffee table arrangement of pale gold-sprayed plastic blossoms

will harmonize with the more informal Chippendale style furniture. (Although some of the finest furniture ever known was made during the eighteenth century, it must be remembered that the designs made for the wealthy were adapted for those less well off. Therefore, although Chippendale furniture may be elaborate, well finished, and quite formal, there is also the "country" variety which is simpler in design and less well-finished, but not lacking in charm.)

FLOWER ARRANGEMENTS FOR THE CHIPPENDALE PERIOD

The Chinese influence that reached its height during this period can be carried out in flower arrangements. The addition of a teakwood base to most of the Oriental bowls and vases of the period emphasize this influence, and contribute to the feeling of the Chippendale period.

Arrangements should be small-scaled and symmetrical; small flowers in muted colors, arranged in bouquet form, are best for small table decorations. Sparseness of chosen and arranged materials typify the restrained formality of this period.

17

The Brothers Adam

As America established its independence from England, the rococo forms fashionable in the Chippendale period declined in popularity. There ensued, in the late eighteenth century and for the first thirty years of the nineteenth century, a revival of Roman Classicism in home furnishings and architecture, a style that was adopted on both sides of the Atlantic Ocean. The association with ancient Rome stemmed from the artifacts then being dug up in Herculaneum and Pompeii. Each discovery was widely publicized and discussed, and the excavations affected every form of the decorative arts.

The strongest single influence in England during this Neoclassic period in design came from the Adam brothers. Robert Adam was an architect whose serene, classic designs were seen in every form of the decorative arts. "Elegance and Utility" was the expression of the day, exemplified also by other outstanding cabinetmakers and designers of this period, such as Hepplewhite and Sheraton. The styles of these two were often so similar that it is sometimes difficult to tell them apart, particularly in styles adapted from one or the other. Both Hepplewhite and Sheraton were influenced by the classic French style of Louis XVI; both designed furniture that was gracefully utilitarian, yet classic in feeling. On the other hand, Adam styles are definitely different—more unified, pure, and yet detailed.

Robert and James Adam were born in Scotland and studied under a French architect in Italy, so it is not difficult to see in what ways they were inspired to create their new style in architecture and furniture. Successful architects at an early age, they not only designed buildings and rooms, but were preoccupied with every detail that was part of each room, including the ceilings (invariably classic and elaborately worked in molded plaster). They also designed carpeting, furniture, and hardware, giving their work a unity found before only in French palaces. The Adams' own style, pure and geometric in line, elaborate in execution, was imposed on the accepted proportions of Georgian furniture.

Every phase of the decorative arts was permeated by the Adam influence. Fabrics, wallpaper, furniture, mantels, and even doorknobs were made in the Adam style from Adam's original designs. Satinwood replaced mahogany, and painted furniture was popular, too.

Most of the Neo-classic pieces were exported to America, for though the Republic had established its independence from England, trade continued. The adapted Adam designs became the new Federal style in America.

Thomas Jefferson's designs for many of his houses show a strong Adam influence. Classicism became the vogue on both sides of the Atlantic, and simplicity and formality of

The blue and white jasperware vases of Josiah Wedgwood are ideal containers for the Neo-classic Adam period, with flowers in shades of blue, also

line were noted in every phase of design. The human figure in Neo-classical form was decoratively incorporated in the Adam designs, appearing in overdoors, and on ceilings, mantels, urns, and plaques.

DECORATIVE ACCESSORIES FOR THE ADAM PERIOD

Ceramics and porcelains underwent an enormous change, due to the Adam influence. Josiah Wedgwood perfected the formula for his ceramic jasper ware body in 1776 and was soon producing plaques, urns, cameos, intaglios, busts, and numerous other objects in jasper ware. It took Wedgwood four years to perfect and make copies of the Portland vase which epitomized the minor art works of the Graeco-Roman period. Mythological subjects were used in profusion on his bas-reliefs, which were often incorporated into Adam-style rooms as plaques set in walls, ceilings, mantels, and furniture. Vases and pots of all sizes and shapes with the same Neo-classical motifs were made, and production of this type of ware has continued to the present day. Other potters in England and France copied the Wedgwood style in Neo-classic pottery and china.

Robert Adam himself designed Neo-classic accessories for his rooms. Pedestals, knife boxes, clock cases, and mirrors

Lilies of the valley are placed in a green jasperware bowl, the white echoing the lilies and acanthus leaves arranged in typical Neo-classic fashion on the bowl

*Dried white statice and blue starflowers are chosen to go
in a Wedgwood sugar bowl of the same colors*

were all made to order from his designs. The Neo-classic
theme was carried out in every element of home decoration,
from the silver to the table linens, and was copied by other
designers.

Antique containers from the Adam period are not hard to
find. Wedgwood urns and boughpots are still available, and
although the antique Adam-period Wedgwood is sometimes
very costly, reproductions have been made continuously by
the Wedgwood company and can be purchased new. Jasper
ware and basalt vases are excellent containers for arrangements of this period providing that the vases are not too
elaborate. Much Wedgwood jasper was made to be a decoration in itself too ornate to be enhanced by addition of flowers.

In England during the last half of the eighteenth century, there was a great interest in floriculture, a pastime which was not to become popular in America until later. For the first time, vases and pots were designed specifically to hold flowers and branches inside the house. The first boughpots, designed by Wedgwood to hold branches, were placed under tables, not on them. Mantel decorations were merely decorative ceramics—urns and vases—and flowers were not used there; instead, they were placed in pots on the hearth.

Silver vase holds lasting arrangement of artificial Queen Anne's lace, chrysanthemums, and dried statice

White lilies with green foliage is a simple enough arrangement
for this blue jasperware vase. The arrangement is placed
on a white marble base for balance in the composition

FLOWER ARRANGEMENTS FOR THE
ADAM PERIOD

The colors used by Robert Adam were soft pastel shades of pink, blue, yellow, and green, to highlight shades of white, which was used most frequently as a background color. Because the Neo-classic period was the first in England to integrate all the decorative arts into a room scheme, for the Adam style it is important that a flower arrangement be kept in the same soft muted colors as those of the room in which it is to be placed. The shape of the container should be in the Classic form, and the composition should be more formal in design than that used in arrangements of the preceding periods.

Formality and painstaking regard for shape were present in all details of the Adam style. Symmetry is an important element to consider in arrangements of this period. Therefore, the topiary may be used with the Neo-classic, as well as silk flowers in the formal triangular-shaped arrangements. Silver urns and bowls designed in Neo-classic style are excellent containers for fresh roses and other garden flowers of formal character.

18

The Louis XVI Period

The Louis XVI style is very strongly characterized by the revival of the Classic lines and motifs brought about by the excavations begun in Herculaneum in 1748. Toward the end of the reign of Louis XV there was a noticeable transition to Neo-classic design in decoration, and the curved lines typical of the early Louis XV style had nearly disappeared by the time Louis XVI became King in 1774. By then, the transition to the Neo-classic was well on the way.

The major difference in furniture was the gradual disappearance of curving, feminine lines and the substitution of more masculine designs. Legs of chairs, tables, and storage furniture became straight and often were fluted to emphasize the verticality. Designs were more symmetrical. Furniture was still festooned and ornamented, but gradually the ornamentation became more delicate in scale, more mathematically symmetrical. Urns and vases were a common motif in marquetry and applied ornament, although flowers and leaves were still used as in the Louis XV style, albeit more

Miniature silk flowers in silver cigarette urn reflect
the symmetrical fashion of Louis XVI

refined and restrained. The emphasis on vertical and horizontal lines typified the style of Louis XVI, making it among the most gracefully designed furniture ever produced in France.

Because of the Revolution, there was little time for marked change in the later Louis XVI style of architecture

*Classic-style urn holds arrangement of artificial anemones,
cabbage roses, and Queen Anne's lace in large formal bouquet*

and furniture. The interiors were Neo-classic in feeling. The
colors were muted and soft: Light blue, rose, taupe, pale
greens and yellows are typical Louis XVI colors.

Ormolu—gilded brass or copper ornamentation—was
used on furniture with much more restraint than formerly.
Furniture was also gilded, painted, or lacquered, and often

was ornamented with Sèvres plaques inset on cabinets and desks.

DECORATIVE ACCESSORIES FOR THE LOUIS XVI PERIOD

By this time in French decoration, the same Classic lines which had revolutionized the output of England's pottery

French bead flowers are ideal lasting arrangements to go with Louis XVI decoration. Flowers are white daisies, blue bachelor's buttons, and red tulips. Container is white porcelain

industry appeared also in French manufactures. Wedgwood had exported great quantities of his jasper ware, basalt, and Queen's ware to France, where jasper plaques and urns were used to decorate some of the Louis XVI furniture, mantels, and walls: French potters copied the Wedgwood style, making simple Classic vases, urns, and pots of all sizes and shapes available as common ornaments. Marble busts of Greek and Roman classic figures were used in profusion in the homes of the noble and the wealthy. Symmetry and simplicity of line dictated the form of sconces, mirrors, and other small accessories.

Although Chinese, Persian, and Indian *objets d'art* were still being imported and used in abundance, the French porcelain industry at Sèvres was flourishing, together with other potteries, and French and Continental pottery and porcelain looked to the Classic for form and inspiration.

FLOWER ARRANGEMENTS FOR THE LOUIS XVI PERIOD

Flower arrangements in this style should be symmetrical and Classic in feeling. Over-lavish containers were no longer the rule; and the Classic lines and pure forms, the simple decoration of creamware and jasper vases (some of which were designed for the express purpose of bringing flowers into the home) give more emphasis to the decorative value of flowers themselves, rather than to the container.

Make flower arrangements in keeping with the Classic elegance of the furniture. Colors used for this period should be soft and muted. Therefore, French silk flowers make ideal

Topiary in a black basalt flower pot is made of plastic
boxwood (See Appendix for methods of making)

*Topiary becomes Louis XVI style when it is placed in
Neo-classic container (See Appendix for methods of making)*

lasting arrangements for this period. Bead flowers in well-
coordinated arrangements are also compatible with this period. Arrangements should be small in scale because the
furniture was more delicate at this time. Fern plantings in
Classic urns, bulb pots, or wall pockets are also appropriate.

19

Hepplewhite and Sheraton

After the Adam brothers adapted the Neo-classic style to English use, there were two noted furniture designers who followed this trend.

George Hepplewhite created a style that became popular toward the close of the eighteenth century. When he died in 1786, his wife Alice carried on his furniture business, publishing his book of designs, which were widely copied.

Hepplewhite's style was more classic than Chippendale's, more simple and severe than the Adams'. His furniture is typified by square, tapering legs, and by shield-back chairs, although the backs were designed as ovals, wheels, hearts, and camel-backs. Despite the modified French influence visible in his early work, we never see the cabriole leg which Chippendale employed so often. Delicate carvings were devices used on Hepplewhite's chairs and settees, and a frequent decoration which sets his work apart from that of other contemporary designers was the Prince of Wales' triple plume. Chests of drawers were usually curved outward, although on his sideboards Hepplewhite made use of both

Silk flowers in muted shades of green and yellow are arranged in creamware gravy boat with classic decorations

Modern silk thread-covered fruit is arranged in eighteenth-century basket for an attractive lasting centerpiece

*Symmetrical arrangement of blueberries, grapes, and pineapple
in a creamware bowl flanked with creamware candlesticks
graces a buffet*

convex and concave curves; the corners are always concave. Inlay was used with great restraint, and satinwood was extensively employed.

Thomas Sheraton, a contemporary of Hepplewhite, carried the Classic revival even further. Unlike Chippendale and Hepplewhite, Sheraton was not a furniture manufacturer, but a designer who sold his designs to cabinetmakers. His work was restrained, featuring graceful lines and good proportions, had very little ornamentation, and was always finely-scaled and sharply-detailed. Sheraton chair backs were rectangular, and the legs were always straight. The kidney-shaped table and desk are typical of his designs.

Both Hepplewhite and Sheraton furniture were imported and the designs adapted and copied in America, though Sheraton was perhaps the more influential.

White dried eranthis plumes and rosebuds made of Thai silk
in a classic-shaped vase are interesting with either
Hepplewhite or Sheraton-style furniture

DECORATIVE ACCESSORIES AND FLOWER
ARRANGEMENTS FOR THE SHERATON
AND HEPPLEWHITE STYLES

In general the styles would be the same as those for any Neo-
classic designers. (*See Adam, Louis XVI.*) Classic-revival

containers and flowers in soft, muted colors are typical of this period in interior design. Simple, restrained arrangements are best, for as this period reached its height before the Victorian era of opulence and over-decoration, it reflected a refinement in home decoration which has yet to be surpassed.

The seashell was a common motif in the inlay of Hepplewhite furniture. This arrangement of dried materials can echo the motif of the furniture

20

Directoire

The French Revolution marked the end of the Louis XVI style, and the furniture of that era fell into disfavor along with all the decorative arts associated with the monarchy. In the years between 1795 and 1799, an interim governing body, called the Directory, was established in Paris; from this comes the name Directoire. The patronage of the aristocracy was now denied to the French cabinetmakers, and many stopped working; while others made plainer, simplified versions of the classic forms they had previously employed in Louis XVI pieces. Their furniture was sold to the politically important and to the newly rich of the time, and though this is considered by many collectors to be the finest furniture ever designed in France, very little was produced, due to the chaotic times and the short span of the period.

Directoire furniture was copied in England for a short time as designers moved toward the more severely Classic forms of a later period. Due mainly to the work of Duncan Phyfe in America, Directoire-influenced designs lasted

*Small brass footed container holds colorful arrangement
of artificial miniature peaches and pittosporum*

longer in this country than elsewhere. The furniture itself is
simple, undecorated, and elegantly proportioned. It later
merged into the grander, bolder French Empire style.

Straight lines, contrasting with restrained double curves
and ornaments such as lyres, swans, stars, and revolutionary
symbols (arrows, fasces, pikes, and Phrygian caps) are typi-

*A creamware bowl with ram's head handles holds symmetrical
arrangement of artificial poppies, blueberries, and baby calliandra*

cal earmarks of the period. Fruitwood, walnut, and oak were
used, rather than mahogany. Painted furniture was also
modish.

DECORATIVE ACCESSORIES AND FLOWER
ARRANGEMENTS FOR THE DIRECTOIRE STYLE

There were few decorative accessories that came out of this
period of upheaval in France. Sèvres could not produce
porcelains without the financial support of the monarchy, and

the brass and bronze workers turned to making military equipment. Therefore Neo-classic vases and urns from England, the earlier Sèvres vases, or Empire urns and vases can be used as accessories with furniture of this period.

Flower arrangements suggested for any of the above periods would be suitable; the flower colors should be light or subdued in hue.

An alabaster urn holds a tall conical arrangement
of dried statice and starflowers

21

French Empire

The Empire period in France is typified by literal adaptations of antique furniture of the Egyptians and Romans. Napoleon sponsored French artisans and directed them to achieve what became known as the Empire style. The grace and dignity of Louis XVI and the Directoire styles were abandoned for a cold, absolute symmetry, with military pomp evident in the ornaments. Sphinxes, griffins, lions, military symbols, and emblems in ormolu and carvings adorned the weighty, bulky furniture. Heavy carved lions' and bears' feet supported tables and cabinets, and swans and eagles were worked into the ponderous furniture in various ways. The "trademarks" of Napoleon, the letter N, the bee, the Empire star, appeared on furniture and in upholstery and draperies. Palm and laurel leaves, cornucopias, fruits, arrows, and torches were also used to embellish the furniture and fabrics.

While the general line of Empire furniture is rectilinear, its bulkiness sets it quite apart from the earlier periods. The Empire craftsmen literally copied archeological motifs, using

Beehive honey pot with fresh flower arrangement
of peach-colored irises, sedum, and honesty

The bear feet on this creamware inkwell are typical of Empire styling. The simple arrangement is of miniature brown-shaded plastic roses and dried baby's-breath

them unaltered; the style's heavy grandeur lost completely the lightness and grace of the designs which had preceded it. It was a totally masculine form of design.

Mahogany, finished in deep, rich red, was favored along with rosewood and ebony; burled wood veneers were also much used. Marble-top tables and chests abounded, with brass ornaments and ormolu coldly applied with mathemati-cal precision.

DECORATIVE ACCESSORIES FOR THE EMPIRE PERIOD

Because of the massive scale of the furniture, the accessories also became larger. Mirrors were flanked with large pilasters and bordered with ormolu mounts on heavy frames. Egyptian motifs, as well as the Napoleonic "N" surrounded by laurel leaves, were often used as decoration on pottery and china; lions' heads were frequently the motifs for handles on urns and pots; white with gold was a common color scheme. Gondolas were a common form for everything from inkwells to dishes. The British, in their usual zeal to emulate French

Bronze inkwell with lion, reflecting the masculine feeling of the Empire period, holds French silk roses in an arrangement for a small table

*Typical Empire style brass-and-glass compote supports
yellow tissue paper roses and wired green paper ivy leaves*

interior design, also began to use the Egyptian motifs. In
both countries the Sphinx was used as a decoration on
ceramics as well as a shape for pottery.

Antique Empire containers for flower arrangements are
still available in antique shops; though as renewed interest

and enthusiasm for what was long considered one of the less beautiful of the French periods has created a demand for Empire furniture, original pieces are disappearing into collections and museums. However, good reproductions or simplified versions (often preferable for use with flowers) are available. Typical forms of this period are urns, footed compotes, and painted tole in square or round shapes.

FLOWER ARRANGEMENTS FOR THE EMPIRE PERIOD

Arrangements in classic-style tureens, urns, and garden containers should be large and symmetrical and composed of larger flowers in order to be in scale with the massive furniture. The colors used during the Empire period were deep and rich, with strong reds, purples, golden yellows, and greens predominating.

22

The American Federal Period— Duncan Phyfe, and Samuel McIntire

The winning of the Revolution saw development of a style of furniture and decoration in America that centered in the New York and New England areas. The Directoire style in France, although short-lived, had great influence on the furniture of this period in America. It was due to the craftsmanship of one furniture designer, Duncan Phyfe, that the simple beauty of Directoire was produced for a longer period in America than in the country in which it had developed.

Duncan Phyfe, influenced also by Sheraton, developed a style that highlighted the Neo-classic period. Therefore, instead of bulky Empire furniture, the combination of graceful, simple Sheraton and Directoire styles that mark the earlier work of Phyfe became the first American design.

The Federal period at it finest is seen in Phyfe's best

Magenta strawflowers and baby's-breath are used together in this small dried arrangement. The container is a modern wooden napkin holder made, however, in the Federal style

cabinetwork. The new nationalism that spread throughout America after the Revolution was evidenced in the constant use of the American eagle as decoration throughout the decorative arts of the period, including furniture. Eagles appeared as drawer pulls, on quilts, and in patriotic pictures. Along with the new nationalism, there arose an avid interest in the Neo-classic, and the architecture of public buildings and homes in America shows how Classic forms were adapted. Thomas Jefferson was deeply interested in the Neo-classic, and designed houses and other structures in the style.

All of the Neo-classic motifs seen in English and French cabinetry at this time show up in Phyfe's work and in the work of those cabinetmakers influenced by him. The acanthus leaf, lyre, oak leaf, wheat ears, scrolls, and reeds are found along with the American eagle. All of the earlier furniture made by Duncan Phyfe between 1790 and 1810 was well-proportioned and elegantly made of carefully chosen mahogany. Eventually Phyfe fell in with the demands of his customers, designing heavier Empire furniture and, later still, the early Victorian type which was then called "French Antique."

Samuel McIntire was a gifted woodcarver of Salem, Massachusetts. He excelled in interpretations of the Adam style, and there were overtones of Sheraton in his work. He did

An American eagle guards this arrangement of chrysanthemums and fall foliage in a painted tin container in drum design

A small table arrangement of American Beauty roses made of flocked plastic and bright blue artificial bachelor's buttons contrasts with an American pressed glass container

architectural carvings of great delicacy and refinement, as well as ornamenting the furniture of his own design. Swags, wheat, bowknots, and other typical ornaments of the period appear on his furniture; but as he did not survive beyond 1811, his work encompassed only the earlier, more delicate style of the Federal period.

DECORATIVE ACCESSORIES AND FLOWER ARRANGEMENTS FOR THE FEDERAL PERIOD

Classical styles with Roman and Greek designs were evident in ceramics and pottery, both imported and local. (The importations from France and England were copied somewhat

141

crudely here.) Flower arrangements were formal, and both pale and deep colors are suitable. Symmetry in arrangement is the same as in the English and Continental arrangements of the time. For the late Federal period, heavier, more robust arrangements are indicated in order to be in scale with the weightier bulk of the furniture and the taste that merged into Victorian.

23

The Shaker Influence on American Furniture Design

In the nineteenth century, for the first time in American history, a style of furniture was launched that stemmed from a religious philosophy. This furniture, in construction and design, is among the best American rural furniture. To understand how this phenomenon came about, it is necessary to understand something of the background of the Shaker sect.

The Shaker philosophy demanded a complete breaking away from worldly interests. Communal living and a resultant demand for furnishings to accommodate this life led to the design and manufacture of furniture that is unique. (This furniture was sold outside the communes, also, and helped support them.) Because of the Shaker tradition of severity and economy in daily life, the furniture made by these people was simple, pure of line, soundly built, and truly functional. This is particularly interesting when one realizes that it took place in the first half of the Victorian period, which produced the fussiest of furniture.

No flowers were allowed in the Shaker household for decorative purposes so colorful plastic vegetables take the place of flowers for the purist who would do as the Shakers did. Every Shaker household had many of these handsome wooden boxes in various sizes (BOX FROM THE COLLECTION OF MR. AND MRS. ROBERT BELFIT)

In the Shaker society, discipline and worship through work was an important aspect of everyday living, and this philosophy led to excellent craftsmanship in every endeavor of the Shaker furniture makers. Perfection and simplicity represented the basic aspects of Shaker lives; shoddiness was not only frowned upon, but simply was not allowed. By denying worldly beauty as expressed in ornamentation, the Shaker craftsmen developed a style of simplicity, cleanliness of line, and functionalism which has not been equalled since their time. Although some of the functional modern furniture of this century reflects a simplicity of approach similar to that of the Shakers, modern manufacture cannot duplicate the handwork and the pure inspiration of Shaker design. Despite its complete lack of decoration, there is warmth and beauty in Shaker furniture, and certainly the quality of construction reflects the personal excellence for which all Shaker craftsmen became famous.

Papier-mâché strawberries fill this Shaker box which originally was made to hold fresh berries. The holes were for ventilation, and the boxes were so made that they fitted neatly into large trays for storage and carrying (BOX FROM THE COLLECTION OF MR. AND MRS. ROBERT BELFIT)

The Shaker philosophy of "beauty rests on utility" is a description of Shaker furniture, and sounds very like the "form follows function" that we hear a hundred years later. However, when comparing a chair by modern designer Charles Eames to one made by the Shakers, one must admit that the spiritual feeling is missing in the new version of functionalism.

Religion permeated every facet of the Shakers' lives, even to the point that the wall colors of their rooms were dictated by the sect. Cabinetmaking took on tremendous importance, and there were definite specifications as to the characteristics the furniture makers should incorporate in their work. Inherently good form, devoid of all "worldly" ornamentation, and the honest use of materials—coupled with the excellence of workmanship that can come only from a complete devotion to one's work—expressed their ultimate goal in furniture design and manufacture.

The Shaker families lived together in groups of thirty to more than one hundred brethren and sisters, and furniture had to be designed to suit large groups of people and to provide worktables which could be used by more than one person at a time. For the first time, ample, well-made, and simple furniture was in use, and quality was not sacrificed for quantity. Shaker furniture is, to this day, perhaps the best designed of institutional furniture. Mother Ann Lee, founder of the Shaker sect, instructed her followers to "provide places for your things, so that you may know where to find them at any time, day or night," with the result that the first built-ins were designed and made by this group.

Compared with other religious movements, the Shakers

This antique Shaker basket bore berry stains and therefore was arranged with artificial blueberries and clusters of green grapes (BASKET FROM THE COLLECTION OF MR. AND MRS. ROBERT BELFIT)

did not last long, but this period produced the finest examples of American rural furniture—straightforward in design and sound of construction. The movement began to die out toward the end of the nineteenth century, due both to the rules of celibacy and to the outside influence of Victorian tastes, which cut down on sales of Shaker furniture and threatened their livelihood.

ACCESSORIES FOR SHAKER DECORATION

No one was idle in the Shaker community; while the men were busy farming and producing furniture, the women made baskets which are outstanding for their beauty and utility. Many of these baskets are still in use today and can sometimes be found at country auctions throughout New

England, Ohio, and New York State. The same fine cabinet-makers who designed and made Shaker furniture also made wooden boxes of various sizes, according to the dictum of a "place for everything." Mortars, various dishes of pewter, and functional wooden containers for kitchen use are also found occasionally. These utensils are distinguishable from other kitchenware of the last century by the excellence of workmanship typical of Shaker manufacture.

No purely decorative accessories appeared in the true Shaker household, for these were excluded completely from Shaker life. Everything allowed in the way of living appurtenances was listed in the Millennial Laws of 1845.

The Shakers were told that bedsteads should be painted green—comfortables should be of a modest color. The blankets for outside spreads could be of blue and white, but could not be checked or stripes. Window shades should be white, or blue, or green, or some other modest color, certainly not red, checked, striped, or flowered.

It is easy to see that a museum curator setting up a typical Shaker room does not have too many decisions to make.

A revival of Shaker design has begun in America, and interest in Shaker furniture, particularly in the New England area, becomes stronger as designers search for a means of uniting modern functional furniture with the warmth and beauty of the old styles. Many Shaker designs are being copied by cabinetmakers who take pride in their work, and Shaker designs are even being copied for mass production.

The serenity of the Shaker room stemmed from a religious philosophy which cannot be a part of modern life, but there is need for some of that quiet aura today. Economy of line and honest use of material without sacrifice of warmth seem to be the qualities which we should borrow from the Shaker designs. Because austerity is not a part of life today, we use Shaker furniture and embellish it by adding those accessories which give warmth and color.

FLOWER ARRANGEMENTS FOR
SHAKER DECORATION

The Shakers did not believe in using any embellishmnets that had no practical function in their homes. Therefore it is safe to assume that a room decorated in pure Shaker style, either authentic or reproduced, would not contain flowers, either fresh or dried. However, there is no reason to-day, when using adaptations of the Shaker style, that flower arrangements as accessories should not be used. The old Shaker boxes are excellent containers for dried arrange-

*Shaker box set on its cover contains a cluster arrangement of dried statice and starflowers (*BOX FROM THE COLLECTION OF MR. AND MRS. ROBERT BELFIT*)*

*A small basket with bachelor's-buttons and pale yellow
daisies would be fitting for an informal dining room, living
room, or any country-style decoration*

ments, and the small baskets made by the Shakers are given
extra beauty and utility when used to contain arrangements
of fruit or bouquets of field flowers. Primitive stoneware,
mugs and small crocks, severely plain pewter ware, and other
simple containers—modern or antique—are suitable.

It is interesting to note that one of the indications of the
decline of the Shaker community was that some of the
members started to grow flowers simply for the enjoyment of
their beauty. It is easy to assume that a sign of how far a
Sister's decadence had advanced was her bringing those
forbidden flowers into the house. Perhaps she, too, saw that
flowers in informal bouquets could only improve this simple
and austere style.

24

The Victorian Period

The Victorian era (1837–1901) embraced many kinds of furniture, and the tastes displayed were often amazing. There was an endless search for novelty, and the advent of mass manufacturing brought forth a new group in Europe and America, the rising middle class, which searched for some way of becoming important. Many of its members emulated the nobility and the rich, and revival after revival took place, with influences including Louis XV and XVI, Gothic, a pseudo-Renaissance, and a host of other partly digested adaptations of Oriental, Venetion, Turkish, Chinese, and other styles.

The new methods made possible by the machine were appreciated by an English designer, Eastlake. He tried to adapt certain Renaissance and medieval forms to the new production methods, but the merits of his originals were distorted by the tasteless copies that followed. William Morris and John Ruskin introduced certain elements of sanity into some of the fashions, but they were not entirely successful. Morris and his group of artists used nature as a source for design for fabrics, wallpapers, and decorative objects.

This Victorian pottery plant holder was spray-painted gold and now holds feathery plastic fern and blue, brown, and white berries

The style known as Early Victorian utilized mahogany, walnut, and other fine woods. Later, oak, burled walnut, and rosewood, as well as other woods with fancy grains, became popular. As indicated earlier, no overall earmarks can be discerned, as the style became diverse with adaptations and revivals.

The furniture of the Victorian era suited those who lived with it. In general it was heavy, ornately carved, showy, and richly upholstered with velvets, plushes, and handmade needlework, often done in flower patterns. Chairs and tables of papier-mâché, with handpainting and often inlaid mother-of-pearl, were popular and are now collectors' items. The Victorian is the last period in which hand carving and fine woods were used for furniture making. The nineteenth century marks the end of furniture making as an art.

Now that we are far enough removed from the Victorian period, we can look upon it with a fairly unprejudiced eye and, as with other periods, adapt and use those things from it which are in good taste and of good design. The oversized dining-room furniture of the Victorian period has not yet enjoyed renewed popularity, but well-made upholstered furniture and small tables and desks are once again being sought after.

It is questionable whether the decorative arts as a domestic pastime will ever again traverse the road of the Victorian era. It was then believed that idleness was sinful, and ladies spent long hours and much eyesight on their china painting, flower making, and embroidery.

DECORATIVE ACCESSORIES FOR THE VICTORIAN PERIOD

The small accessories of the Victorian era are mostly elaborate and overdecorated. Large iron urns, ornamented with grapevines and flowers, are typical outdoor decorations and are now used on porches and terraces. Papier-mâché boxes, painted and inlaid, can still be found occasionally at auctions or in antique shops. Mantel vases, used in pairs, were the showpieces of the Victorian parlor. They were usually of the flare type, and the white cottage flare vases are good flower containers if they lack the usual Victorian ornamentation.

The English glass industry grew to large proportions during Victoria's reign, and many of the English cut glass

Victorian daguerreotype frames hold pressed flower pictures. The photographs were removed and fabric used for background

pieces are excellent Victorian flower containers. The bell jar, which can almost be called a symbol of the Victorian era, covered and protected arrangements made from every material imaginable. Some of the original arrangements can still be found intact, and one can still buy bell glasses in several sizes for one's own arrangements of dried flowers and foliage. This is an ideal way to display fragile dried arrangements, because they are protected from dust and deterioration.

Cut crystal, majolica, terra cotta, Staffordshire pottery, stone china, Parian, luster ware, Bristol glass, and bone china were but a few of the types of materials from which dishes and display pieces were made. The more numerous and elaborate pieces one owned, the better, and every home had a whatnot on which to display the overflow from the china cabinet. Some of the most beautiful chinaware and pottery, as well as some of the ugliest, was made then.

Eclectic was the descriptive word for Victorian tastes, for nearly every decorative period that had come before was revived, often in somewhat exaggerated form. Therefore, the flower arranger has only to go to the nineteenth century to find containers in the Gothic, Oriental, Neo-classic, and rococo styles—or any other type of container to suit any other period. There is enough variety for anyone's taste.

Decorations for china and pottery of the Victorian era included gilding, lustering, enamelling, and dipping. Coats-of-arms and crests were used by everyone entitled to them,

Huge arrangement sports many kinds of flowers in a bronze vase made in France in the Victorian period

*Papier-mâché box of the mid-Victorian period holds an
abundance of green grapes and foliage, all artificial*

and even by some who were not. Fashionable colors were
dark blue, apple green, yellow, turquoise, lavender, purple,
and deep red. Bird, fruit, and flower motifs were hand-
painted or transfer-printed. A good many dishes were decorated with a process which used lace for decoration.* Dishes
by Spode and Copeland in the Imari patterns of red, gold,

---

* The lace was laid on and materials poured over which adhered
to it. The lace was then burned away in firing, leaving the design
in porcelain.

and cobalt blue after the Oriental designs, became popular in the Victorian era and have been in demand ever since by those who enjoy elaborate tableware.

FLOWER ARRANGEMENTS FOR THE VICTORIAN PERIOD

It would be difficult to discuss Victorian flower arrangements without first some exploration of what flowers meant in the Victorian way of life. Although America's heritage of gardening and love of flowers had come from England, where gardening was a firmly established avocation, lack of time and interest in the esthetic, plus a puritanical denial of art and beauty for their own sake, had postponed the development of any widespread interest in flowers on the American continent. The early settlers of America had little time for floriculture. It is was not until the time of Queen Victoria that the first American publication of a periodical devoted expressly to horticulture was printed; but once this interest was established, it soon became widespread, and floriculture as a business became profitable. Flowers and the use of them in any form for home decoration are almost synonomous with the Victorian era: they are its symbol.

Large, showy blossoms became popular, and the geranium and the dahlia were great favorites of the day. The zinnia was offered by an American seedsman in 1865, and it, too, quickly became popular. It suited the Victorians very well, for it was—in that early version—bright, large, and showy.

Every genteel lady learned flower painting, and seedsmen often depended upon the art of flower drawing for their

*These flower prints were a method of advertising seeds in
the nineteenth century, and had blossoms listed under the print.
This kind of composition can be adapted for arrangements*

sales. Flower prints, the forerunner of today's seed catalogue, became as popular in America as they were in England and France. Young ladies took courses in flower painting, and the drawing masters of the day provided stencils so that the less talented pupils could be happy with the results of their efforts. The eager pupils also copied flowers from books that were published expressly for that purpose. No originality was necessary. Publishers brought out sentimental flower prints for the home in vast quantities, often accompanied by some sentimental message.

The hothouse rose was still a novelty, but the lace-trimmed, beribboned bouquet from the florist was the most

Transfer-printed Gothic revival commode is useful
for a foliage arrangement

159

Pressed dried pansies, balloon flowers, and violets in a Victorian frame provide a permanent flower decoration with antique velvet mat keyed to color of the flowers

exciting gift a Victorian swain could send his inamorata. When she dressed to go to a party, the Victorian lady wore a camellia in her hair and carried a bouquet. There could not be too many flowers in the house, in the garden, or on the person.

This was the age, also, of the artificial flower. Feathers, wax, shells, paper, silk—all were materials from which floral decorations for the home were made. Some of these were beautiful, and many of them have survived to become museum pieces. Fabrics were embroidered with flowers, and floral forms dominated the needlework of the period.

*The blue and gold paisley border on this Victorian bowl is
enhanced by the selection of dark blue eranthis plumes
and blue-dyed teazles*

Wax flower arrangements and other imitations of real
flowers were for the well-to-do, but less affluent ladies could
satisfy their need for embellishing their homes by making
pressed, dried arrangements. Everyone, including children,
collected flowers and plants and pressed them. These materials were then arranged in bouquets and wreaths and
framed to adorn the walls of Victorian parlors. Enormous
dried bouquets decorated the foyers, sun porches, and solar-
iums. Huge groupings of house plants made it possible for
the avid gardener to pursue his interest during the winter
months.

Flowers covered every form of the decorative arts in the Victorian era. Furniture was carved with garlands of ornate flowers. Glass vases were often painted with flowers, and china-painting became a hobby that consumed the time and talent of thousands of Victorian ladies. Shiploads of British and French china were imported unadorned and then decorated, mainly with flowers, at home.

Because of the Victorian interest in flowers and gardening, production of lawn furniture and ornamentation became a flourishing business. Iron gates and fences in floral designs were popular, and ornate urns, garden seats, and statuary were used by everyone. Everything became adorned with floral designs, and every conceivable material was used for them. Flowers were modeled of leather, seeds, and fabric, and cones were arranged in ornate designs and framed for hanging in the parlor. Flowers made from the hair of dead relatives were arranged in frames, often surrounding a photograph of the departed.

The above ought to inspire any number of Victorian period arrangements. Lots and lots of flowers in elaborate containers create a Victorian mood. Large blossoms, bright colors, and enormous bouquets are appropriate. Artificial flowers of any material, and expecially large paper ones, are excellent adjuncts to Victorian decoration.

25

The Japanese Influence on Western Interior Design

Although the Chinese influence on Western interior decoration and architecture had been felt during several of the historic periods in varying degrees, the influence of Japan appeared rather late. Trade with Japan did not exist until late in the nineteenth century, when foreigners were allowed to come in, and began to expand in the twentieth century. In Europe and America, before that time, the words "Chinese" and "Japanese" were interchangeable in many minds so far as decoration and works of art were concerned. With the advent of Japanese trade there came the realization that the Japanese had something different and important to offer the decorative arts. Flower arranging was one of the areas where the Japanese influence was, and still is, being felt.

The traditional Japanese room, built of unpainted wood, was devoid of color and definite pattern. The flower arrangement in its own alcove, or *tokonoma,* was often the only decorative focal point in the room, and was usually accompanied by one excellent example of calligraphy hung on the wall. The arrangement was a living painting, with flowers used as pigments; it changed with the seasons and reflected the Japanese religion and life of the time.

In order to understand more fully the importance the Japanese attach to flower arranging, it is necessary to realize that the *tokonoma* was designed originally for esthetic enjoyment and religious exercise—in other words, as the family altar. Twice a day it was the family gathering place for worship. Although most of its religious significance has now disappeared, the *tokonoma* is still felt to be somewhat sacred, demonstrating the high regard that the Japanese hold for nature in all its forms.

Ikebana, the Japanese term for the art of flower arrangement, has been in use for many centuries, but dates so far back in history that it is difficult to name a specific time when the art was not an important aspect of Japanese life. It is known, however, that contests for excellence in flower arranging began in the late sixteenth century. For the Japanese, flower arranging is part of Shinto worship of nature and it has been on a par with any of the other fine arts in Japan for many centuries. It is practised by both men and women, but the most noted flower arrangers and teachers are usually men.

There are many schools of Japanese flower arranging, some of them dating back hundreds of years. The arrangements follow prescribed symbolic designs reflecting the seasons and certain other types of natural phenomena. Any material that grows can be used. In a land so small and

This Japanese vase, with its Western interpretation of
Japanese flower arrangement, has a painted design of
irises. The same flower repeated in the arrangement is
interesting, but not fussy

overpopulated, every branch, stone, and flower is highly thought of and used to its best advantage to create works of art.

The influence of Japan upon the Western world and its flower arranging began as soon as travelers had visited Japan and saw how highly developed the art had become in that country. This occurred about the end of the nineteenth century.

The Japanese influence was felt in many other areas of the decorative arts by the twentieth century. The renewed interest in artists' prints stemmed directly from the discovery of Japanese woodblock color prints. In a book published in 1906, *Color Prints of Japan*, Western artists whose work was influenced were given a chapter. Dante Gabriel Rossetti, James McNeill Whistler, and Aubrey Beardsley are all discussed and their work shown. There is no question but that the Art Nouveau style (see page 172), based on nature and natural objects, stemmed directly from the nineteenth-century Japanese influence on all art. A major aspect of that influence was in flower arranging. Beauty found in assymetry and in art imitating nature became the guiding principle of Art Nouveau.

An important aspect of Japanese flower arranging—and indeed, of all Japanese art—is that the visual balance that may be found in an apparent irregularity is a higher form of art than that which appears symmetrical to the human eye. Visual balance in primitive art is achieved by a regular symmetrical arrangement of like sizes, colors, masses, and lines. In assymetrical designs, on the other hand, balance is achieved by the use of irregularity, of weighing small against large, line against line. To the Japanese, and to many Westerners today, this is more beautiful.

The organization of garden clubs in England and America is said to be a direct result of the impact of the Japanese emphasis on flower arrangement as a highly developed art form rather than as a mere decoration for the home. Western garden club flower-judging rules display an artificiality when compared with the rules governing Japanese flower

A low dish arrangement using apple blossoms and several irises has a peaceful quality. Flowers that blossom at the same time were used together for harmony

arranging, and at times it has been felt that an overemphasis of line and technique has hindered rather than helped the development of flower arranging as an art form in America and England. Furthermore, an art so steeped in religion, philosophy, and tradition can hardly be copied or taught in the amount of time Westerners are willing to devote to it. We display other forms of art, achieve our color and pattern in other ways in the home.

The respect for the handmade in a world that had begun to pride itself on the ability to mass produce items was the inspiration that drove artists toward Art Nouveau and the styling of glassware, pottery, and furniture of great individuality. They tried to hold the applied arts in the same high regard with which the fine arts were viewed, and by giving these artisans a new respect for nature, the Japanse influence was responsible for inaugurating Art Nouveau style.

DECORATIVE ACCESSORIES AND FLOWER ARRANGEMENTS IN THE JAPANESE STYLE

The Japanese distinguish between formal and informal arrangements. The *rikkwa* and *ten-chi-jin* styles are formal, while the *nageire* style is informal. Because the latter is the most natural, it is the one which appeals most to Westerners and has become the most popular one in recent years for those interested in studying and learning the techniques of Japanese flower arranging. In *nageire,* the emphasis is on the unforced look, or the "thrown in" technique of arranging flowers.

The *rikkwa* style, on the other hand, can best be described

The beginning of Art Nouveau with its strong Japanese influence can be seen in this bronze vase. Two lilies, with some buds about to open, were used for this arrangement

as "a little garden within the house." It usually includes several species of trees and flowers symbolizing the landscape. It is from this type of arrangement that the "Japanese dish garden," complete with Oriental figures, bridges, and miniature teahouses, was derived. These "dish gardens" could be seen in almost every American home in the 1920s. The *rikkwa* arrangement includes all the symbolic elements of the Japanese garden—the pine tree, the flowers, the rocks, stones, and water. This form of arrangement is probably one of the oldest types, but it is now less popular in Japan than formerly.

The *ten-chi-jin,* or heaven-man-earth, style is a relatively new school of Japanese flower arranging which dates from the middle of the nineteenth century. Its basic form consists of three branches of various lengths. The longest branch is called *ten* (heaven); the medium branch, *jin* (man); and the shortest branch, *chi* (earth). The heaven branch is placed in the middle of the vase, the man branch at one side, and the earth branch in front of the heaven one, thus forming an irregular triangle. Any other material added to this arrangement is subordinated to these three major lines.

Ikebana of today is quite different from the Japanese flower arrangement of the past. Western influence on Japan, while not as strong as the reverse influence, began to be felt at the beginning of the twentieth century. Western flowers were introduced, and the pin holder, called a *kenzan* by the Japanese, began a new school of Japanese flower arranging called *moribana.* The metal flower holder, with many needle points to hold flowers upright, enabled the flower arranger to put flowers in a shallow dish. The *moribana* style may be formal or informal, and it allows the arranger a great deal of freedom. From the *moribana* style has come the modern school of flower arrangement in Japan, which has evolved into the school of the abstract. Leading Japanese flower arrangers of the abstract school are treated with as much respect and admiration as the best contemporary painters are in the West. Their arrangements are frequently closer to sculpture than to flower arrangements as we know them, and they reveal amazing ingenuity.

Plant materials found in Japanese arrangements are as unlimited as those found in nature. Live branches—or dried ones—leaves, and other plant materials are sparingly combined with a few meticulously chosen flowers. Color is secondary to form, and colors usually reflect the season of the year. The containers used for holding the arrangements are quite varied, but highly decorated containers are seldom used. The container is considered an integral part of the design, and it is therefore chosen with careful thought as to its shape, color, and general design. Containers for *rikkwa* and *nageire* arrangements are tall; those for *rikkwa* are wide-mouthed. *Moribana* containers are shallow and may be of various shapes. Pottery, baskets, bronze urns, and vases are all used by the Japanese, often for specific flower arranging styles—though more liberty is permitted in the modern schools of flower arranging and containers may now be of almost any material.

26

Art Nouveau

A period of decoration highly original in concept and execution was developed at the end of the nineteenth century. Condemned by stuffy Victorians as decadent and tasteless, the Art Nouveau movement encompassed all of the decorative and graphic arts. Although it lasted only a short time, its influence was wide, and recently the style has been revived. For the first time in the history of the arts, there were movements in England and France to bring together the finest craftsmen and designers in order to unify the designs of buildings, furniture, wallpapers, fabrics, ceramics, metalwork, and glass. That the useful should be integrated with the decorative in the highest manner was the aim of the young artists who turned their attention away from the fine arts and toward designs for articles which would be both beautiful and useful and would encompass every facet of life.

Art Nouveau was more than a style—it was a philosophy, from which came a renaissance of carefully designed, handmade articles for the home. The roots of this new movement were in the rococo of the Victorian nineteenth century, but the ideas and the approach were new. The experimentation with ceramic glazes, the use of glass as an art material, and the concept of many good artists working together to achieve unity, whether in glassmaking or the graphic arts, led to original designs which are easily discernible from those of any other period. The artists working in this period were strongly influenced by the Japanese, and from this inspiration came the typical Art Nouveau line. In Art Nouveau design, line was the most important aspect. Flowing and rhythmic, it gave a feeling of movement to everything from

A porcelain vase, handmade in the Netherlands, holds one large paper poppy

*Orange pottery vase of typical Art Nouveau shape is
filled with large feather flowers*

jewelry to tables. The flower shape was seen everywhere in
the decorative arts, and the study of nature became a neces-
sity for anyone designing articles for the home in the new
fashion. The exotic and the esthetic were of major importance; the languorous line that symbolizes Art Nouveau
could be found in every article that had to do with daily
living.

In actuality, the Art Nouveau movement lasted only
about twenty years. World War I changed life so completely

The shape of this Art Nouveau glass vase dictates shape of
arrangement, which consists of plastic cornflowers and roses

Pottery plate and cup with blue and red Art Nouveau border
has the theme carried out in an arrangement of blue
bachelor's buttons

Rookwood pottery bottle uses gracefully curved inch plant spray to accent its own curves (BOTTLE FROM THE COLLECTION OF MR. & MRS. RICHARD N. FRIED)

that it necessitated a new expression in the arts. The ornamental, fluid lines disappeared, and the rigid, stark, modern style of the 1920s, '30s, and '40s became dominant. During the past ten years collectors have become increasingly interested in this brief but important movement.

Because the Art Nouveau movement lasted such a short time, most of the well-designed furniture and art objects are already owned by museums and collectors. In addition, although they worked in a period when mass production was

*Beleek jug of the Art Nouveau period with arrangement of dried flowers has a focal point of a large red tulip, dried in silica gel (*JUG FROM THE COLLECTION OF MR. & MRS. RICHARD N. FRIED)

the rule rather than the exception, the best Art Nouveau craftsmen designed and made their products by hand. Even though some craftsmen's groups were large, the work they did was so refined that it was comparatively expensive.

Furniture is less symbolic of the Art Nouveau movement than small products such as ceramics, glass, engravings, and etchings. The fine leaded glass made by Louis Comfort Tiffany has now become prohibitively expensive, but there is other art glass for the flower arranger to own and use.

SMALL DECORATIVE ACCESSORIES FOR ART NOUVEAU DESIGN

Art Nouveau design permeated every area of the decorative arts. Its distinctive style of flowing assymetrical lines of plant, flower, and shell shapes was found in everything from lighting fixtures to door hardware, from furniture to drapery fabrics. However, since so many Art Nouveau vases are flower-shaped or otherwise designed or decorated as artistic entities, many may not make good containers for conventional flower arrangements, and care must be given to their selection.

Some of the interesting types of glass vases were made by

Blue overlay container with silver-sprayed artificial blue roses, has an aura of Art Nouveau

Emile Gallé, by the Daum brothers who were influenced by Gallé, and Emile Michel (all three in France); by Karl Koepping in Germany; and, of course, Tiffany in America. Each handled glass in his own way, but all employed the fluid lines and design forms of Art Nouveau.

There was a renewed interest in ceramics during this movement, and guilds were formed in many countries of Europe for the purpose of experimenting with clay and bone china. Often, as at the Rozenburg firm in the Netherlands, for instance, one artist would design and shape the body which another would decorate by hand. There was wide experimentation in pottery design.

In pottery, porcelain, and glass, the new design produced beautiful new fluid shapes. The glazes and colors of glassware and pottery reflected the excitement of the artists who designed and made them.

Even though the products of this period are limited in number, many Art Nouveau vases offer a fascinating and lively range of colors, lines, and forms.

FLOWER ARRANGEMENTS IN ART NOUVEAU STYLE

In contrast to the massive bouquets of the Victorian era, Art Nouveau flower arrangements were more stylized, primarily because of the Japanese influence. Plant material used for these arrangements should be interesting in line and texture; flowers should be employed as individual pieces rather than as groups or in large bouquets.

The same fluid lines of the Art Nouveau container should

The wonderful glaze on Hungarian Art Nouveau pottery looks like iridescent fish scales. Three peacock feathers take the place of flowers in this arrangement

be extended into the arrangement. Root, tree trunk, and flower shapes will dictate naturalistic arrangements; nicely shaped branches from trees and flowering shrubs stripped bare of foliage (or partly denuded) can often provide the proper lines for backing floral material. When a vase is decorated with a particular flower pattern (nasturtium, lily, poppy, and iris were frequent motifs) use the same flower in the arrangement, if possible. Because of the strong Japanese influence in Art Nouveau, the use of only a few flowers, a single branch, or a few twigs——most carefully placed—— is most appropriate.

Real lilies and their foliage are gracefully arranged in an orange-color Art Nouveau pottery vase

27

The Modern Functional Style

At the close of the Art Nouveau period, designers broke away from nature as the inspiration for their art and began to design buildings and furniture in which form followed function. De Stijl in Holland, strongly influenced by the painter Mondrian, rebelled against the flowing lines of Art Nouveau and employed functional, assymetrical designs reflecting the machine age.

In America, the architectural and furniture designs of Frank Lloyd Wright dominated the early twentieth century and, spreading across the world, led to many variations on the modern concept which not only eschewed extraneous decoration but, often, decoration of any kind. In the past, only Shaker furniture had followed the same basic idea of simplicity. The stark, undecorated look of both styles is similar although the inspirations are widely different.

In the twentieth century, wood has been used less and less in furniture construction. Designers used modern materials such as tubular steel, laminated plywood, glass, and leather.

Charles Eames and Eero Saarinen used aluminum, molded plastic, and molded plywood. Function and ease of maintenance are most important, and beauty is often of secondary importance, although a pleasing appearance is usually found in furniture conceived by the leading designers.

Severity and lack of pattern in the materials used in buildings and furnishings characterized the more "classic" modern designs of the 1930s. Natural and rough-textured materials in solid colors were used for upholstery and drapery fabrics, and carpeting was usually of a single solid color. Very few decorative ornaments were used in the home, and simplicity, rather than opulence, dominated the mood of interior decoration. This style of decorating is still in use in commercial buildings, where ease of upkeep is essential, and the functional look continues to dominate our architecture to a large extent.

In the first third of this century there was still a strong interest in handcrafted decorations, and, ironically, much of the furniture by the best modern designers was fashioned or at least finished by hand. Ceramics and glassware from the Scandinavian countries suited modern interiors because their simplicity and weight were compatible with the simple uncluttered backgrounds. Handwoven Scandinavian fabrics and rugs were imported and influenced American designers to a great extent. Extraneous decoration was avoided in all phases of interior design and everything that was not of this century was excluded. For a while, even a painting from another era was thought to be out of place, and only abstract and modern paintings were used.

The twentieth-century modern design movement was

*This is a typical S-shape arrangement in the modern
style. A square green pottery pillow vase with yellow
African daisies and willow foliage accent the lines*

international, and designers everywhere in the world created
their own versions of the functional. Dominating the movement were America, Sweden, Finland, Germany, and the
Netherlands in architecture and furniture design; France led
in painting and sculpture.

DECORATIVE ACCESSORIES OF THE MODERN FUNCTIONAL STYLE

Swedish crystal and glass, utterly simple in form but elegant in material and craftsmanship, are typical of this period. Handwrought silver and pewter containers with little or no extraneous decoration can be used to create a more formal feeling. In decorative accessories, as in all else, the beauty of pure modern design stems from the material used and the form in which the article was made rather than in applied decoration. Because there is no pattern to conflict with a carefully composed flower arrangement in a modern setting, the arrangement becomes a dominant feature in a severely modern interior. Because of the starkness of modern architecture and decor, large houseplants and tall, monochromatic flower arrangements requiring little care have become the customary accessories for this type of room.

The machine age has dominated all facets of the decorative arts. Easy-to-care-for items for the home led to today's use of stainless steel flatware, platters, serving dishes, and pitchers. New synthetic fibers have revolutionized the fabric industry. Until very recently, the most simple design was considered the most beautiful, and the fact that an article was washable, unbreakable, did not tarnish, and had a function in the home was a major basis for its purchase. Hand-thrown pottery was made with little or no applied decoration, but glazes and textures were more interesting. The architectural look in glassware became important, for without cutting and designs or decoration to depend on, shape was all that was left. Form had beome the single most impor-

Foliage, as well as large houseplants, were used frequently as a severe decoration with nineteen-thirties functional modern furnishings

tant aspect of design in the flower container, as in furniture and architecture.

FLOWER ARRANGEMENTS FOR THE MODERN FUNCTIONAL STYLE

After the enormous, uncontrolled bouquets of the Victorian period and the languid, but carefully controlled, arrangements of the Art Nouveau period, modern arrangements of the 1940s became more abstract and stiff. Severely modern ceramics and glassware called for stark plant materials, and unusual materials from all over the world were used. Many of these "modernistic" arrangements had a contrived look.

Exotic materials and ideas from countries such as Hawaii and Japan, where flower arranging has so long been considered essential to everyday life, became available after World War II and modern arrangements began to soften.

As a whole, modern arrangements as a class remain simple of line and starkly contrived, and they frequently employ unusual material.

Colors used in modern flower arrangements are usually bright, contrasting with white or monochromatic backgrounds. The use of exotic plant material for these arrangements is widespread. Dried materials have enjoyed a renewed popularity, and desert branches, dried pods of all sorts, and other materials of unusual shapes and colors are available to the flower arranger by mail or through local suppliers.

The four red tulip buds in this black container reflect
the economical use of material in modern arrangements
The earlier influence of the Japanese led to many simple,
effective arrangements such as this

28

Eclectic Interior Design

If there is one truism in the decorative arts at the present time, it is that the day of handicrafts is, indeed, over. What cannot be made by machine in sufficient quantity to fill the demands of an affluent and discriminating market is simply not made. As it has become obvious that the ease of maintenance associated with functional modern decoration does not preclude the need for beauty and pattern in everyday life, there has been a widespread hunger for those objects which were made by hand in the past.

Since the beginning of interior decoration as a profession, there has been an interest in and a market for antiques, and certain periods adapted features and furniture designs of previous periods. Antique collecting has heretofore been a hobby for the rich or for the particularly knowledgeable amateur. It is now a craze which pervades the middle and upper classes of both America and Europe, making the antiques trade one of the fastest growing businesses today. The only problem is lack of merchandise.

The good designs of every historic period have been so extensively copied that Chippendale, Sheraton, Duncan Phyfe, and other names have become household words during the middle of this century. Although period styles rise or fall in favor, at present almost any furniture, decorative accessory, or utilitarian object that was made in the past (but particularly the better examples of each period), are in enormous demand. Museums attempt to purchase the best examples of past decorative periods in order to preserve them, but frequently museums are outbid by private collec-

Stoneware dish holds paper flowers (African daisies, poppy, and zinnia) made from directions in a Victorian book. The arrangement is designed in a modern style, however

tors searching for excellence in design and construction. The value of good antiques in today's economy seems to increase faster than that of many other investments. The law of "supply and demand" applies to the antique market and, because supply is limited, demand and price increase.

The first era in which exact reproductions of different styles were used to any extent was the late nineteenth century. Those who disdained the Victorian style, with its varied adaptations and vulgarizations, turned to earlier styles. Newly rich families in America who had not inherited antiques purchased a semblance of family ancestry and heritage by collecting European and American antiques. This practice was by no means as widespread then as it has become in the 1960s.

A blending of decorative periods of various compatible designs which reflect our heritage (personal or otherwise) has been one of the most successful accomplishments of today's best-trained interior designers. They draw from the important periods of the past and blend or contrast fine antiques with furniture of good modern design to create an atmosphere that combines color and warmth with elegance while still maintaining the ease of upkeep which has been the major contribution of the functionalists. This has been termed Eclectic interior design.

"Eclectic" means that the best is selected from a number of sources and blended together to create a compatible new whole. It seems a good term for the new approach to decoration outlined above. It is probably a reaction to the coldness of the functional modern approach of the early part of this century as well as to the museum-like copying of period

Red and white double petunias in Chinese lotus dish

rooms that went before. Home-owners seem to have found that there is no enjoyment in caring for that which is not esthetically satisfying. The same brass accessories that were put away in basements or stored in attics at the end of the Victorian period are now back in the living room—and still need a weekly polishing. Turned and carved wood eschewed by functionalists as a "dust catcher" is more highly prized today than when it was new. One criterion of how high the bids on a piece of furniture will rise at auction may be the handcarving on it. Anything handmade sells today.

The mixture of old and new furniture and art objects from all corners of the earth, representing many periods of decoration, reflects the society in which we live just as much as any previous style reflected its time. New methods of travel and communications have brought the continents so close together that there is less and less of a national style. Only that which was designed in the past is "typically French" or "typically English". Because communication is so immediate today, art has become a personal, rather than national, endeavor. It does not seem likely that there will ever again be a group such as the Dutch School or the French Impressionists, and certainly the day of the patronage of kings to enourage a national style is over.

DECORATIVE ACCESSORIES AND FLOWER ARRANGEMENTS FOR ECLECTIC DESIGN

Flower arranging, along with the other decorative arts, seems to be undergoing a kind of revolution. Significant is the advent of finely wrought plastic flowers and, although they have a minimum of publicity, plastic flower companies are today enormously successful. Good polyethlene flowers and foliage have quietly been accepted by many leading interior designers as an important part of room decoration. By the use of plastic flower arrangements, a room may be enhanced with semi-permanent arrangements on high shelves or in other places so inaccessible as to preclude the use of fresh flowers. (Of course, when they are to be viewed closely, fresh flowers are to be preferred.)

For today's Eclectic decor, any container of a harmonious

*A Victorian frame holds pressed-flower arrangement made
in the naturalistic style of late Art Nouveau*

A Victorian toothbrush holder now is graced with bright Japanese paper flowers in an interesting eclectic-modern arrangement

design, in a color chosen to enhance the overall color scheme of the room, may be used. The flowers can now be arranged in any style which looks good, although the present trend seems to be toward loose, informal bouquets similar to those of the eighteenth century; they are colorful and not overly time-consuming. More formal bouquets, such as are seen at flower show competitions, are also in keeping.

Scale is the most important single factor in flower arranging for today's Eclectic style. A properly scaled arrangement, with colors chosen to complement a room's decoration, set in one of the lovely old containers that we collect today (or in a reproduction of one), can give warmth and a lived-in look to today's homes.

Modern arrangement of dried okra, artichokes, and poppy
seed pods is placed in a Beleek vase of the Art Nouveau period

Directions for Making Topiaries of Louis XIV Period

DIRECTIONS FOR MAKING
BALL-SHAPED TOPIARIES

MATERIALS NEEDED: 5-pound bag of plaster of Paris; one wood dowel, ½-inch diameter, cut to length of 24 inches; 20 sprays of plastic spruce; roll of florist's tape; 12-inch length of florist's wire; cardboard paint pot; water; spoon for mixing; styrofoam ball 5-inch diameter; "Accent" floral spray paint, moss green; small wire cutter; small ceramic flower container.

STEP 1: Mix half of plaster of Paris with water in paint pot according to directions on package. When plaster has thickened and all lumps have disappeared, pour into flower container to within 1 inch of rim.

STEP 2: Place dowel upright in center of container and hold it firmly until plaster sets. The dowel should stand alone after about 5 minutes. Let plaster harden for at least 1 hour. Check several times to make certain that dowel is vertical.

STEP 3: Beginning at top of dowel, wind florist's tape tightly around the dowel, pulling gently and winding downward until the entire dowel is covered. Fasten end of florist's tape with a drop of Elmer's Glue-All.

STEP 4. Spray styrofoam ball with green spray paint and let dry. Push styrofoam ball onto the top of the dowel until dowel reaches the exact center of the ball.

STEP 5: Wind florist's tape tightly around entire length of wire, then cut wire into 4 equal sections. Hold 4 sections of wire spaced evenly around sides of dowel at the top 2 inches below styrofoam ball so that the top ends of the wires touch the ball and that there is ½ inch left at the bottom where wire is being held. Still holding ends of wires, curve tops of wires outward so that they will look like thin branches. Wrap florist's tape around the dowel and all 4 wires to hold in place. Continue winding tape to bottom of dowel; cut it off, then fasten end inside of rim of container with a drop of Elmer's Glue-All.

STEP 6: Using wire cutters, cut all sprays of spruce from main branches. Trim to uniform lengths.

STEP 7: Poke stem ends of spruce sprays into styrofoam ball, starting at the dowel end and working up. Reserve six sprays. Be certain that sprays are inserted into the styrofoam ball so that when the topiary is finished it will be perfectly symmetrical and look the same from all sides.

STEP 8: Mix 1 cup of plaster of Paris with water and carefully spoon into top of container so as to prevent getting any plaster on the dowel. As plaster hardens, arrange remainder of spruce sprays in it around the top of the container so that they branch outward. This will soften the arrangement and give it a more balanced look.

DIRECTIONS FOR MAKING
THREE-TIERED TOPIARY

MATERIALS NEEDED: Styrofoam cone 10 inches in height; "Accent" spray paint, moss green; wood dowel, ½-inch diameter, cut to 12-inch length; dark brown spray paint; twelve branches of plastic boxwood; 5-pound bag of plaster of Paris; water; cardboard paint pot; small package of sphagnum moss; 4 thin dry twigs three inches long; spoon for mixing plaster; small inexpensive footed container about the size of a sherbet glass; feathered peacock; kitchen knife.

STEP 1: Spray dowel with brown paint and let dry.

STEP 2: Cut ½ inch from top of styrofoam cone, using kitchen knife. Cut cone horizontally into 3 equal sections, being certain to cut straight through. Spray each section on all sides with green paint and let dry.

STEP 3: Mix 2 cups of plaster of Paris with 1 cup water in paint pot until all lumps have disappeared and consistency is thick. Spoon into container and stand dowel upright in center of container. Hold dowel for 5 minutes or until the plaster hardens enough so that dowel stands vertically by itself. Before plaster sets completely, spread moss over the top of the container and push into the plaster slightly so that it will adhere. All plaster should be hidden.

STEP 4: Using scissors, cut boxwood sprigs off main stem and cut each sprig in half, leaving about ½ inch of stem on each sprig. If you do not have enough stem on the ends of each sprig, trim a few leaves off the stem end. (It will look as though you have an enormous amount of boxwood sprigs when all branches are trimmed, but you will need every bit.) Poke the stem ends of the sprigs into the 3 sections of the styrofoam cone, covering all the surfaces of each section, so that no styrofoam is visible. On the largest section, poke in 4 twigs ½ inch from the center of the underside and space twigs evenly so that they will form a square around the dowel when the styrofoam is placed on it. (See photograph.)

STEP 5: Push the largest section of styrofoam onto the dowel, making certain that the dowel goes straight through the center of the styrofoam section; push down until the twigs rest on the top of the plaster of Paris. The twigs may need a little adjusting so that they will support the styrofoam evenly to keep it from slipping. They should look as much like natural roots as possible. Push the second section of styrofoam onto the dowel. Insert the dowel only halfway through the top section.

STEP 6: Place peacock near top of first tier for focal point and color interest, inserting the wires attached to the feet in the styrofoam.

Bibliography

Andrews, Edward D. and F. *Religion in Wood: A Book of Shaker Furniture.* Bloomington: Indiana University Press, 1966.

Aronson, Joseph. *The Encyclopedia of Furniture.* New York: Crown Publishers, 1938.

Better Homes and Gardens. *Flower Arranging.* New York: Meredith Press, 1965.

Bjerkoe, Ethel Hall. *Decorating For and With Antiques.* New York: Doubleday & Company, Inc., 1950.

Butler, Joseph T. *American Antiques 1800–1900: A Collector's History and Guide.* New York: The Odyssey Press, Inc., 1965.

Chippendale, Thomas. *The Gentleman and Cabinet Maker's Director.* London: Dover Publications, Inc., 1966.

Clements, Julia. *ABC of Flower Arranging.* Princeton: D. Van Nostrand Co., Inc., 1963.

Clements, Julia. *Flower Arranging.* London: C. Arthur Pearson, Ltd., 1963.

Clifford, Chandler Robbins. *Period Furnishings: An Encyclopedia of Historical Furniture, Decorations and Furnishings.* New York: Clifford & Lawton, 1914.

Costantino, Ruth T. *How to Know French Antiques.* New York: New American Library, Inc., 1961

Drepperd, Carl W. *First Reader for Antique Collectors.* New York: Doubleday & Company, Inc., 1954.

Fastnedge, Ralph, *English Furniture Styles: From 1500–1830.* Harmonsworth: Penguin Books, Ltd., 1955.

Bibliography

Hinckley, F. L. *A Directory of Antique Furniture: The Authentic Classification of European and American Designs for Professionals and Connoisseurs.* New York: Crown Publishers, 1953.

Hughes, Therle. *Old English Furniture.* New York: The Macmillan Co., 1963.

Hughes, Therle. *Small Decorative Antiques.* London: Lutterworth Press, 1959.

Kahle, Katharine Morrison. *An Outline of Period Furniture.* New York: G. P. Putnam's Sons, 1929.

Kimerley, W. L. *How to Know Period Styles in Furniture.* Grand Rapids: Periodical Publishing Co., 1917.

Lancaster, Clay. *The Japanese Influence in America.* New York: Walton H. Rawls, 1963.

Lichten, Frances M. *Decorative Art of Victoria's Era.* New York: Charles Scribner's Sons, 1950.

McBride, Robert Medill. *A Treasury of Antiques.* New York: Robert M. McBride & Company, 1939.

McBride, Robert Medill. *Furnishing With Antiques.* New York: Robert M. McBride & Company, 1939.

McClinton, Katharine Morrison. *The Complete Book of American Country Antiques.* New York: Coward-McCann, Inc., 1967.

Marcus, Margaret F. *Period Flower Arrangement.* New York: M. Barrows & Company, Inc., 1952.

Morse, Frances Clary. *Furniture of the Olden Time.* New York: The Macmillan Company, 1936.

Museum of Modern Art. *Art Nouveau: Art and Design at the Turn of the Century.* New York: The Museum of Modern Art, 1959.

Museum of Modern Art. *Introduction to Twentieth Century Design from the Collection of the Museum of Modern Art.* New York: The Museum of Modern Art, 1959.

Musgrave, Clifford. *Adam and Hepplewhite and Other Neo-Classical Furniture.* New York: Taplinger Publishing Co., Inc., 1966.

Ormsbee, Thomas Hamilton. *Care and Repair of Antiques.* New York: Robert M. McBride & Company, 1949.

Parsons, Frank Alvah. *Interior Decoration, Its Principles and Practices.* New York: Doubleday, Page and Co., 1929.

Plumb, J. H. *The Horizon Book of the Renaissance.* New York: American Heritage Publishing Co., Inc., 1961.

Bibliography

Rheims, Maurice. *The Flowering of Art Nouveau*. New York: Harry N. Abrams, Inc., 1966.

Richie, Donald, and Weatherby, M. (eds.). *The Masters' Book of Ikebana*. Tokyo: Bijutsu Shuppan-Sha, Publishers, 1966.

Rogers, Joyce. *Flower Arranging*. London: Paul Hamlyn Ltd., 1964.

Rutt, Anna Hong. *The Art of Flower and Foliage Arrangement*. New York: The Macmillan Co., 1958.

Sato, Shozo. *The Art of Arranging Flowers: A Complete Guide to Japanese Ikebana*. New York: Harry N. Abrams, Inc., 1965.

Savage, George. *A Concise History of Interior Decoration*. New York: Grosset & Dunlap, Inc., 1966.

Schmutzler, Robert. *Art Nouveau*. New York: Harry N. Abrams, Inc., 1964.

Spry, Constance. *Flower Decoration*. London: J. M. Dent and Sons, Ltd., 1934.

Townsend, Reginald T. (ed.). *The Book of Building and Interior Decoration*. Garden City: Doubleday, Page and Co., 1923.

Truman, Nevil. *Historic Furnishing*. New York: Pitman Publishing Corp., 1950.

Van Arsdale, Lurelle, and Drepperd, Carl W. *New Geography of American Antiques*. New York: Guild Award Books, 1961.

Viaux Jacqueline. *French Furniture*. New York: G. P. Putnam's Sons, 1964.

Williamson, Scott Graham. *The American Craftsman*. New York: Crown Publishers, Inc., 1949.

Index

Index

Index